»»—→ EX LIBRIS ←—««

_____

Heirloom Modern

HOMES FILLED WITH OBJECTS
BOUGHT, BEQUEATHED, BELOVED,
AND WORTH HANDING DOWN

HOLLISTER H. HOVEY

PHOTOGRAPHS BY
PORTER L. HOVEY

RIZZOLI
NEW YORK

New York · Paris · London · Milan

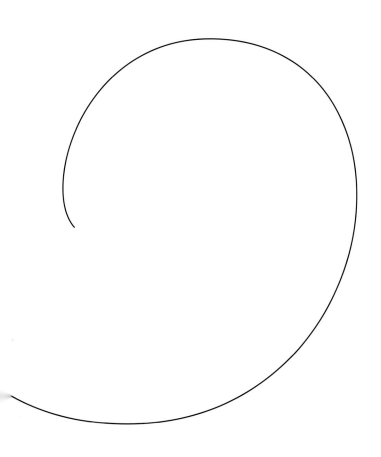

»»—→ FOR LANA ←—««

LIVING LEGACY

Our mom, Lana, a brilliant and creative woman but not one for going on and on quoting poems or speeches, would occasionally pull one out when she felt my little sister, Porter, and I needed inspirational prodding to don kimonos at Christmas, throw on boys' madras Brooks Brothers blazers for kindergarten, or make life-size papier-mâché leopards in third-grade art class while the other kids made chickens and pigs.

"Remember girls, 'To thine ownself be true.' Shakespeare gave that advice. He was a very smart man."

She meant that for us as individuals, but also as it applied to our family's way of life. It came through in our family traditions, how we dressed, the foods we ate, and how we decorated our home. If we loved watching black-and-white movies filled with flapper dresses and white linen, traveling far and wide to shop for things we couldn't find at home, and eating artichokes with abandon, then we should keep doing those things for the rest of our lives. We didn't have to try to keep up with the Joneses. In fact, if you asked Mom, it was imperative that we forge our own path and identity. If we wanted to reference popular trends, that was okay, but we should always add our own special twist to stand out from the crowd.

It was a confident view, and it played out beautifully since our parents' aesthetic considerations seemed to have dribbled down right to our DNA. Kids often rebel and grow into a taste and style that hovers on an opposite pole to that of their parents, but as children, Porter and I loved our mom and dad's furniture and art from "exotic" places like New York, Paris, and Africa. Everything in our house had fun stories or once belonged to people who seemed keen on adventure, travel, and exploration. We wondered, who wouldn't want to come home to the grown-up, indoor version of *Babar*, *Curious George*, and *The Jungle Book*?

The lessons in taste and style we didn't absorb through the amniotic fluid were doled out as a series of rules that could have been taken from Strunk & White, if those two men had concerned themselves with clothing and interiors instead of grammar and writing. Mix high and low, and classics with ethnic pieces. Stick to natural fibers and materials. Buy heritage brands instead of the new copies. Embrace color. And never, ever wear cheap shoes.

Our mom was born after World War II in Lincoln, Nebraska, to Vinona Mae Halverson, a housewife with Hollywood starlet looks, and Peter Jacobs, a strapping, hardworking Burlington Northern Railroad switchman who loved trains, fishing, and gardening. Mom and her little sister, Rita, ran wild and horsed around outside with the neighborhood kids, loved rock and roll and sports, and studied like crazy. Their parents, the loves of each other's lives, flirted with each other openly well past middle age.

Mom's childhood read like the American Dream, but the whole while, she was reading *Vogue* and *Seventeen*, spending every cent of her baby-sitting money on clothes, fantasizing about a life in New York and the far-flung locales featured on the pages of those magazines.

Determined to make something of herself outside of Nebraska, she applied to a highly coveted internship at *Mademoiselle*, the most intellectual of Condé Nast's women's books, known for featuring the writing of everyone from Truman Capote to Flannery O'Connor, and also to a post-grad publishing course at Radcliffe. Radcliffe said yes. So at twenty-one, she headed off to Cambridge, Massachusetts—her first time away from home. Those six weeks changed her life. We watched a lot of Nebraska football throughout our lives, but our mom's "college stories" were all wonderful anecdotes from that summer that seemed to play out like happier versions of *Love Story*. As her summer at Radcliffe wound down, she applied for jobs and landed one in New York—at *Mademoiselle.*

Our dad, Porter Lamson Hovey, had a wildly different upbringing. His boyhood was full of frenetic movement back and forth from California to Seattle to New York as his parents divorced and remarried. He eventually settled with his mom and his brother and sisters in Old Westbury, the tiny community in Long Island polo country and where his mom's second husband lived. After boarding school and college, he went on an ocean voyage where he escorted thirty heads of cattle to the Philippines and negotiated the purchase of a racehorse in Australia before arriving in South Africa. There, he spent a month on an Afrikaner farm and then made his way along the Indian Ocean and to Cape Town, Durban, and Johannesburg. He spent two years in the early 1970s with his brother and stepbrother running a Bolivian gold mine.

After meeting at a New York party, Mom and Dad married the day after Valentine's Day in 1975 and celebrated with friends and relatives at his mother's sprawling Park Avenue apartment with peach walls, herringbone wood floors, and a perfect mix of contemporary pieces and antiques. They honeymooned in Paris, where the marriage nearly ended because Dad thought Mom was buying too many French magazines. He got over it, and they came home and found a one bedroom on 63rd Street and Madison Avenue.

Dad had furnished his uptown bachelor pad with his stepfather's oval leather-top desk and a nineteenth-century Russian brass bed, which had both been relegated to a chicken coop in Old Westbury. Those pieces went into the new apartment, along with our mom's Deco-inspired chrome and glass dining room table, a peach couch, minimalist side chairs, a collection of baskets they picked up at local flea markets, and a black-and-ivory Moroccan rug that used to lie in his mother's Southampton beach house.

They developed a great social rhythm: Dad played rugby in Central Park on Mondays, they went to dinner with friends or entertained Wednesday through Saturday, and they brunched together on Sundays. When they stayed home, they'd watch TV, read, and needlepoint pillows and chair coverings in patterns Mom had designed.

By '77, Mom was getting homesick, so our parents headed to Lincoln, Nebraska, to settle down and make a family. They moved into a two-story, redbrick, Georgian-style house with a red tile roof and detached garage. All the furniture from their old place came with them, including a trove of beautiful wallpapers from Dad's mother: hand-painted black lacquer for the kitchen, a bold, geometric peach and black for the hallway, and a floral Chinoiserie for the master bedroom.

I was born a year later.

Lincoln gave my parents the Midwestern calm, kindness, and safety that Mom had remembered from her youth. But with one step into that house, they were immediately transported 1,300 miles away to the life they'd first known together in New York.

Porter and I had wonderful, culturally rich childhoods in Lincoln and then Kansas City, where we moved when I was five. We went to museums and the ballet, ate croissants and drank hot chocolate from delicate teapots on our birthdays, and opened our presents on Christmas Eve like Grandma Vi's Norwegian family did. We spent hours with our mom—from the stroller through our college years—combing antique stores and flea markets for new treasures.

Our parents always wanted us to leave the Midwest—at least for a while. We both did, and for the last seven years, Porter and I have lived together in a loft in Williamsburg, Brooklyn, that's filled with the mirrors, knickknacks, pillows, and paintings that our parents started with in New York, along with taxidermy, vintage luggage, zebra-skin rugs, and countless other pieces that we've picked up from eBay and shops around Brooklyn and during our travels. We've added our own style to the mix, reinterpreting the lessons our parents taught us through a modern lens with a different set of influences and experiences.

Our home has become a living autobiography, tracing our family's roots and telling the story of our childhoods and experiences as adults. If we have our own children someday, we hope that they will love these pieces as we do—not for any kind of monetary value, but because of the memories and stories they relay. To us, that's "heirloom" in the most modern sense.

←« ←«
Our grandmother, Armene, hosted our parents' 1975 wedding reception in her Park Avenue apartment. This picture shows Mom and Dad relaxing in her master bedroom after the ceremony. Our parents used wallpaper in the same geometric pattern as our grandmother's curtains to decorate the walls of our first family home in Lincoln, Nebraska.

»→
Grandpa Bill, our dad's father, was born to an old Kansas City family that moved to California when he was a boy. He remained loyal to the West Coast for the rest of his life, and spent over four decades there with his third wife and soul mate, Ann Gay. He died in 2007 in Pasadena at age 92.

←⇐

Our Grandma Vi died before
Porter and I were born, and
it broke our mom's heart
that we never got to meet
the woman who gave her
and our Aunt Rita their
independent spirits and
fierce loyalty to each other.
Here she is at our parents'
wedding reception in 1975.

14

»→

Our dad's half-sister, Carey Clark, graduated from the Rhode Island School of Design and has painted her entire adult life. She's been lucky to have ample studio space in all of her New York apartments. This picture shows her in her loft on LaGuardia Place in 1979.

»→

Our dad and his younger brother, Peter, play a fierce game of backgammon at their father's Pasadena home in the early '70s. Dad used to play for hours when we were kids, and our grandma still hosts weekly games with her friends.

←≪

Our parents stayed at the Hôtel Plaza Athénée on their honeymoon in Paris. On that trip, our mom snapped up the peach, floral Hermès scarf that hangs framed over our living room mantle.

←≪

Our mom always staged elaborate Christmas and Easter photo shoots. This is an outtake of Porter from the 1985 Easter session in our living room in Lincoln. The day bed in the background belonged to our dad's mother.

»→

On Christmas eve, our mom
would dress us in vintage
kimonos from her collection
to wear while we opened
our presents. Here I am in
1982 sitting next to the desk
that Dad rescued from a
chicken coop, which now
sits in our Brooklyn loft.

»→

Our grandmother and dad
sit in the living room of
her apartment in the early
1970s. The painting over
the couch now hangs in the
dining room of her classic
six on the Upper East Side,
against glazed walls that
would have almost exactly
matched the sofa seen here.

»→

All of Grandpa Bill and Ann
Gay's homes were decorated
in bright chintz patterns
reflecting the expansive
gardens in their neighborhood in Pasadena. Here
they are with Porter in the
living room of their home in
Pasadena in the late 1980s.

PORTER HOVEY &
HOLLISTER HOVEY

We moved into a new house in Mission Hills, Kansas, a country-club-laden suburb of Kansas City, Missouri, when I was ten, and Porter, five. Throughout the entire—and very, very long—house-hunting process, Mom joyously riled us up with plans for the wall color of our beautiful new bedrooms. Porter's would be a pale yellow ("Blondes look great in that color," she said), and mine would be pale pink, like a proper little girl's room. But our new house wasn't very beautiful at all. The surrounding neighborhood was lovely, full of mansions, rolling hills, fountains, and manicured gardens, but the outside of ours looked like a drab, 1960s stone ranch house with color accents as exciting as mud. The inside resembled a disco with wall-to-wall carpet, as if the people who lived there before had continued to throw key parties well into the mid-'80s. The baby-blue kitchen had yellowed linoleum, which, like almost all the walls throughout the house, was full of gold speckles.

Somehow, though, Mom saw past the glitz and envisioned our new home as a lovely, airy cottage. The carpet was the first thing to go, then the gold, flocked wallpaper and the wall of mirrors in the master bedroom. Porter got that room. Our parents figured they would convert the attic for themselves, so they gave me the two other first-floor bedrooms (one, ivory with loads of orange Formica, the other, the color of a rotted olive), and knocked out the wall in between. They whitewashed all the floors and ripped out the wallpaper.

Porter did get her yellow bedroom, with a mahogany four-poster bed, chintz bedding, French doors on the closets, dark wood Art Deco night stands with marble tops, and a mantel that held family photos—just like an English cottage. She loved her room and took particular pride that she, as the little sister, had been first in line for a renovation. One night, though, I woke to her screams from down the hall and ran in to suss out the problem. She sat up sobbing, terrified. "What's wrong?" "The wallpaper monster came!" Sob. Sob. "Bolts of lightning came out of his fingers and he put the gold wallpaper back over my yellow walls!" I turned on the light and tried to reassure her that she was still surrounded in buttery beauty, but she cried for the next half hour, terrified of the prospect of going back to the room as it had been before. Looks like Mom had created her own little wallpaper monster.

Our mom died in 2002 and, a few years later, our father remarried and decided to move into his new wife's place. Before he sold our old house, he let the two of us come and take the pieces we loved most back to Brooklyn. Turns out, we loved a lot of things "most." Today, the framed Hermès scarf Mom bought on their honeymoon to Paris hangs over our mantel, just a few feet from the 1933 life-size portrait of a hunter, his dog, gun, and cigarette that Mom and Porter found at one of our favorite Kansas City antique stores. The Venetian mirror she and our dad bought from an estate sale at the Governor's Mansion in Lincoln hangs in our entry, flanked by our dad's six beloved Scottish military prints that we found in a Kansas City flea market. The leather-topped desk he rescued from the chicken coop for his bachelor pad fills our living room corner. The pillows our parents needlepointed when they lived in New York sit on our Plexiglas and faux-ostrich-skin chairs that we found in a mid-century furniture shop in Manhattan. An Italian ceramic ottoman that they found in a store in Nebraska, lugged to

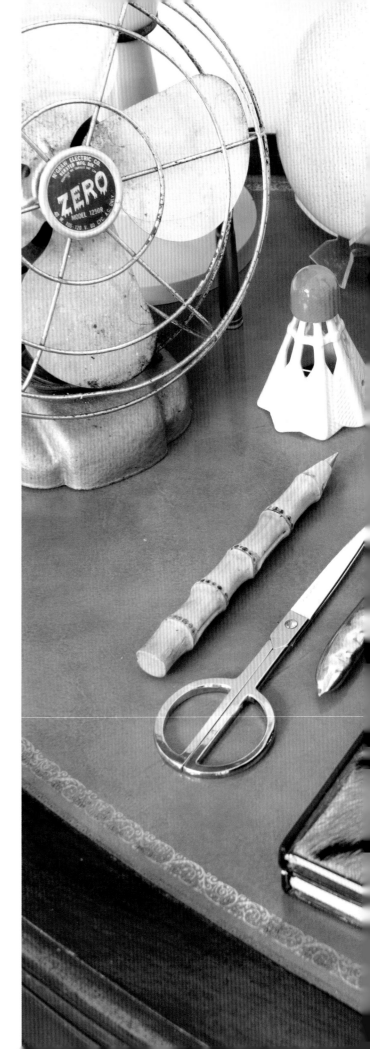

New York, back to Lincoln, and then Kansas City is there, too. And that's just a start.

Just like our mom, we're constantly on the hunt for new finds with their own varied histories to give our family's old pieces new context. Understanding the mantra that you'll never find what you want when you're looking for it, we integrate our shopping into our daily lives, like brushing our teeth or showering. Unlike many expert junk shop scroungers, I'm not much of a picker. I go in more like an eagle and swoop down the moment I see ostrich skin, an old military ribbon, or a pith helmet. Once I went out for a Saturday coffee run and came back with hand-painted, 1940s Louis Vuitton luggage. Transactions typically transpire like that, in a matter of seconds, without a hem, a haw, or a modicum of regret, especially if Porter, the slightly more measured of us two, isn't there to stop me. When we travel, we tend to seek out places that allow us to escape from work and our jobs into a heightened, more beautiful (if not just different) reality that very closely mirrors our favorite weekends at home—with entirely new antiques to swoop over and scoop up. There's the canvas and leather top-hat box and the Ottoman epaulettes and gold-threaded ceremonial belts we found in Istanbul; the vintage riding hats, small, striped trunk, and gigantic Anglo-Indian porcupine quill box from London; loads of old books with wonderful Bauhaus fonts, an old miner's hat, and a spelunking belt from Prague; an old German anatomy chart from Copenhagen; toy soldiers from Paris; a stoneware platter from Marrakesh and the taxidermied black bear head we plucked from the wall of a used-book store in Camden, Maine.

We think our mom would be proud to see her things—objects that represented her and her experiences with our dad so perfectly—updated through her daughters' eyes and tastes that have been honed through our time in New York and the trips abroad that she always wanted us to experience. And we know she'd be thrilled to see that we've created our own special home out of the big beige box we moved into.

←《←《

Our mom, Lana, bought the Hermès scarf that hangs over our living room mantel in Paris in 1975. She designed the needlepoint pillow patterns and enlisted Dad to help with the stitching during their nights home as newlyweds in New York City.

←《

Our tabletops all hold mementoes of our childhood, like the ceramic shuttlecock from the Nelson-Atkins Museum of Art in Kansas City, the leopard-print egg that our aunt Rita painted for me as an Easter gift in 1981, and a silver envelope box that Porter made in silver-smithing class in high school.

←⤛
Our mom's beloved
Venetian mirror and Dad's
favorite Scottish military
prints surround our
growing taxidermy menag-
erie that includes swans, a
scarlet ibis, a baby alligator,
and a zebra-skin rug.

⤜→
Our mom chose Ceralene
A. Raynaud Limoges "Les
Oiseaux" porcelain as her
wedding china and always
incorporated naturalist
touches—like nautilus and
sea urchin shells and palm
trees—into her decor. We've
continued that tradition.

REGINA

←‹‹

Porter and I incorporate vintage and junk store shopping into our daily rituals the way others work in coffee runs, gas refueling, or trips to the grocery store. But I've also found countless treasures online. This Napoleonic watercolor was one of my first purchases on eBay.

←‹‹

The scarlet ibis that I found on Craigslist punctuates our taxidermy collection with a burst of crimson and infuses an exotic freshness into the space.

←⋘

Our dad always loved toy soldiers but preferred to collect full regiments. We love grouping one-offs who have lost their comrades for unexpected mixes of color, costume, and politics. We seek out new soldiers whenever we travel and found these in London.

←⋘

Orange Hermès boxes that held our mom's scarves provide a great pop of color in our seating area. Mom always treated her tiny Anglo-Indian porcupine quill box as a treasure, so when I saw a larger one at Henry Gregory on Portobello Road, I made the investment and thought she'd be proud.

←«

Our parents found this Italian ceramic ottoman on an early trip to Lincoln, Nebraska, then lugged it back to New York where they were living at the time. Porter and I found the industrial steel table (to the right) on the street by our apartment for twenty dollars. A slab of marble that Grandpa Pete rescued from an old Nebraska bar fits perfectly on top.

»→

When our parents left New York for Lincoln in the late 1970s, they opened a shop selling ethnic and natural-fiber clothing, including vintage silk kimonos. We keep this one from the store out as a colorful counterpoint to our parents' Martha Washington shell-patterned needlepoint chair and the nineteenth-century top-hat box I brought back from Istanbul.

←«

Porter still uses the marble-topped nightstands from her childhood bedroom, which today hold our dad's dented, monogrammed silver baby cup and family photos. Porter has filled the charm bracelet our grandpa Bill gave her in high school with mementos from our travels, a gold nugget from the Bolivian mine our dad ran in the 1970s, her baby ring, and a camera to celebrate her photography.

←«

Our dad rescued this leather-topped desk that belonged to his stepfather, Avy, from a chicken coop in Old Westbury, New York, where he grew up. His mom had it restored as a wedding gift to our parents, and it was always one of their favorite pieces.

RITA & AL OSGOOD

In 1971, Mom moved from a West Village studio to a tiny one-bedroom apartment on East 32nd Street. Her little sister, Rita Rae, landed an internship in the city that summer and came to sleep on the couch for the next four months. Of course, they also shopped for furniture. "That's where we started our lifelong passion of going to antique stores and vintage shops," our aunt said.

They snapped up a circular gold-leaf mirror that would eventually hang in my childhood bedroom, the chrome and glass table that would later hold dinners at Mom and Dad's first apartment, our house in Lincoln, and then our first house in Kansas City, and a set of red-and-white English stoneware plates that Mom thought would look great arranged over a fireplace.

As a little girl, Auntie Rae watched our mom pore over fashion magazines, and—as little sisters are wont to do—picked up the habit herself. With an apartment to decorate, the sisters added *Architectural Digest* and *House Beautiful* to their line-up of periodical references. From that summer on, our aunt started (and never stopped) reading almost every single decorating magazine she could get her hands on and soon formed her own style, similar to our mom's but with the color knob dialed all the way up.

In 1995, she met and married Alfred Osgood. Much like our dad, Al spent his youth in prep school and living in elegant East Coast houses (albeit in Maryland and Maine instead of New York). His mom had always favored traditional Colonial American antiques and the classic Williamsburg, Virginia, aesthetic with light walls and Persian rugs. That influence rubbed off on Al, who decorated his own homes in a style closely mirroring the interiors he'd grown up with in Chevy Chase and the family's four-generation summer house in Camden.

As a married couple, Auntie Rae and Al decided to start fresh on the house front, so they found a few acres along Maryland's Eastern Shore and built a two-story, gray-shingled, Colonial-style house with two screened-in porches that overlook the water from both the first and second floors.

The newlyweds also had to marry two very separate styles inside their new home. Al had rooms full of American antiques from his family, but our aunt had no interest living with traditional white walls. She envisioned his heirlooms against backdrops of vibrant hues, creating a setting for these things unlike anything our uncle saw growing up. The office is a bright royal blue, the living room, hibiscus coral, and the master bedroom, an intense peachy cantaloupe. It's a wonderful effect that adds freshness to their home and enhances the natural beauty of the garden and water views that they have from all but one room in the house.

Our aunt has always been incredible with arts and crafts. She took up oil painting a few years back and emerged from her class with a perfectly rendered Dutch-style still life of blue-and-white china against black; she creates gingerbread houses that look like Chinese pagodas, complete with hand-painted blue-and-white fondant urns out front; and she completely transformed Al's old china closet, painting it with bright corals and blues in intricate detail to match and complement his mother's export china service. "To me, that china closet brings a lot of our families' heritage together," my aunt said. "It holds Al's family's porcelain and silver, as well as my mom's prized etched water glasses and a set of ivory napkin rings that my dad bought me in London."

She and Al have also filled their home with small, deeply sentimental objects, which live alongside art from Maine and along the Eastern Shore. Many of the small personal items in the house—including a collection of Hardy fishing reels and New Brunswick and English salmon flies—belonged to Al's great uncle, Dr. Edward Paine from Winslow, Maine, a man he considers "one of the great heroes" of his life. Ned, as he was known, was an avid hunter and fisherman, who on visits back to Maine would often venture out to catch a salmon or shoot a deer with his good friend and fellow sportsman, Leon Leonwood Bean—whom most people know by his initials, L. L.

Now that both she and Al are retired, our aunt is steadfast in her efforts to keep the house alive and evolving. Every month she pores over *House Beautiful* and *Architectural Digest* for inspiration, just as she has since that summer in New York with our mom. And about once a year, one room gets a wild new hue, so all of the mementoes inside can be seen in an entirely new light.

←《←《←《
This bookcase in the office of our aunt Rita and uncle Al's waterfront home on Maryland's Eastern Shore holds the flies and fishing reels that belonged to Al's hero, his uncle Ned (who was also one of L. L. Bean's best friends and hunting buddies), as well as Al's collection of decoys by Eastern Shore carvers.

←《←《
Almost all of the American antiques in the house come from Al's family, who decorated their homes in Chevy Chase, Maryland, and Camden, Maine, in the style of Williamsburg, Virginia. Our aunt added her touch to their aesthetic by incorporating shocking bursts of color throughout their home.

》》→
Photos of Grandpa Pete, Grandma Vi, and Al's parents sit on the side table that once belonged to Al's mother.

←‒⟪

An oil painting by one of Al's brothers depicting the family's summer home in Maine hangs in the sunroom above our aunt's collection of needlepoint pillows.

⟫‒→

Our aunt painted Al's old dining room hutch in bright corals and blues in intricate detail to complement his mother's export china service. It also holds Al's family's silver, Grandma Vi's prized etched water glasses, and a set of ivory napkin rings that Grandpa Pete bought for our aunt in London.

»»→

Al grew up with all the white wicker furniture that sits on their ground-floor, screened-in porch overlooking the pool and waterfront. Our aunt painted the colonial chair a bright celery green to add a pop of color outside.

»»→

A Maine landscape by one of Al's brothers hangs behind a bee box that belonged to Al's Uncle Ned. Bee boxes like this were used to help hunters locate wild honeybee hives.

←─⋘

A tassel that our aunt found in Florence hangs from Al's paternal grandfather's highboy, which holds a model Hooper's Island Draketail boat that our aunt built, as well as a photo of her mom and a pewter julep cup holding guinea hen feathers.

←─⋘

Al's mother, who studied art at Smith, painted the watercolors of birch trees that hang above a table holding two powder flasks and a scrimshaw powder horn from Al's Uncle Ned and an early photo of Al's son, Hudson.

←⫷

Washington, D.C., portrait artist Jean Reasoner sketched this pastel of Uncle Al as a toddler that hangs in the couple's bedroom above a formal photo from his early years in the U.S. Marine Corps (bottom right). An African beaded bracelet that our aunt bought from our parents' store in Lincoln, Nebraska, sits near Grandpa Pete's railroad watch.

⫸→

A photo of Grandma Vi holding Karolyn Kay, her and Grandpa Pete's first baby, sits on a side table in the sunroom. Karolyn died in Grandma Vi's arms when she was four. Our mom and aunt, shown with their parents in the photo on the right, never knew their big sister.

ARMENE MILLIKEN

After our dad and his siblings went off to college and finished their schooling, our eternally glamorous grandmother moved off Long Island and into "the city." She kept her Southampton beach house as a weekend escape through most of the 1990s, but has been fiercely loyal to the Upper East Side for four decades. During her time in Manhattan, she lived in four different stately buildings sprinkled within a three-avenue zone near Central Park.

I was seven when I visited New York for the first time and saw one of her Manhattan apartments, a large two bedroom in the Hotel Delmonico, the building at 59th Street and Park Avenue that housed Christie's auction house at the time and where Bob Dylan reportedly turned the Beatles on to marijuana in 1964. To me, this apartment looked like the home of a great adventuress—laden with mementoes of her trips with friends and husbands across all the world's continents besides Antarctica. There were zebra-skin rugs from Kenya, chests from China and India, and cups of cigarette holders like the ones the stylish flappers used in the opening credits of *Mystery!*

By the time I moved to New York in 2000, she was living in a new apartment, the classic six where she still resides today. It epitomizes everything I associate with Upper East Side living: crown moldings, glazed walls, and herringbone floors. Each of the rooms boasts a dramatically different color palette, but they all share common features that crop up wherever she lives: a nearly pious devotion to symmetry; plush, beautifully upholstered seating options; and scores of highly personal prints and paintings.

Just like the apartment I remembered visiting as a child and the one where she threw our parents' wedding reception in 1975, this—beyond being spectacularly beautiful—is a perfect place to throw a very proper party.

Mimi, as we grandkids call her, has always had a true gift for arranging people and making social events memorable. After each family dinner, held every few months, we gather in her large living room amid peach glazed walls, a twelve-foot-high Chinese lacquer screen from her last husband's family, and a near-life-size portrait of her in an elegant, black silk cheongsam. This room invites guests to mingle in groups or to steal away into deep, intimate conversations in one of the many two-to-three-person seating arrangements. Within those four walls, we can gather around the games table, where she plays bridge and backgammon with friends several times a week, sink into the overstuffed floral couches or leopard-print French chairs, gather by the fireplace on the loveseat or pink rope-motif ottoman, or sit nicely on the Louis XIV bench or side chairs at the far end of the room.

When we head into her dining room—which features bright green glazed walls, a green-and-brown rug depicting mischievous monkeys that she brought back from India, and two white ceramic parrots perched on Plexiglas stands—she tries her best to arrange us man-woman-man-woman around the large circular leather-topped table. Over plates of lamb or meatloaf and lots of wine, we tell family stories, gingerly address politics, and analyze the latest society and celebrity gossip.

Afterward, we retire by the fireplace in her library, which has a carpet needlepointed in ivory with tiny patterns of green leaves and walls covered in padded celadon and ivory silk fabric. The equestrian oil paintings and prints that fill the walls of this room

hearken back to her years in Old Westbury spent with her second husband Averell "Avy" Clark's family of polo and horse breeding enthusiasts. The built-in bookcases on either side of the desk hold scores of family photos and two framed *Life* magazine covers: one of Avy in full fighter-pilot gear standing next to the P-47 Thunderbolt that he flew during World War II, the other of Mimi, in a sparkling green evening gown and long white gloves on the way to a Seattle party in 1955.

Mimi honed her taste working with decorators like Betty Sherrill and then helping her friends outfit their New York apartments and summer homes in the Hamptons. Her years of travel and vacations—and time spent in many of America's most beautiful properties had a deep impact, too. "As we grew up, we watched her take in the influences of friends and decorators around her—and then use her own formal abilities to make our family homes and her New York apartments really beautiful," Carey Clark, our dad's youngest half sister, said.

Alida Morgan, whose father, Eddie, was one of Mimi's closest friends for over three decades, feels that our grandmother has an immense talent for creating spaces that make everyone feel welcome. "She has an extreme feminine touch, but it's grounded by masculine pieces with sporting and hunting themes and absolute symmetry," she said. "Both men and women are equally comfortable in her homes."

While Mimi maintains her active social life and continues to entertain throughout the week, she insists that she no longer loves shopping for decor these days. In fact, she's been dispersing much of her furniture to her children and grandchildren for decades—and helping us all arrange it. Porter and I have a bamboo trunk that matches a smaller one in her library, Aunt Carey has chairs and a large antelope-print wool rug, and our Uncle Peter and Aunt Pat in Connecticut have a floral needlepoint rug covering their entire living room.

We're all so lucky that our matriarch is still around, as vivacious, flirtatious, and tasteful as ever. Our family dinners give us a great reason to get dressed up and catch up. Frankly, it's a wonderful arrangement.

←⫷←⫷

In the 1960s, artist Maria de Kammerer captured the style of our cheongsam-clad grandmother Armene perfectly: worldly, elegant, and beautiful. De Kammerer painted a series of portraits for the family and many hang in the peach living room of her classic six on the Upper East Side.

←⫷

Mimi, as we call our grandmother, displays her orange-and-white porcelain, a wedding gift, inside two mirror-image built-in arched bookcases in the dining room. Much of our love of incorporating animals into our decor comes from her.

←《← ←《

At family dinners, Mimi tries her best to arrange guests man-woman-man-woman around the large, circular leather-topped table. Over plates of lamb or meatloaf and lots of wine, we tell family stories, gingerly address politics, and vocally analyze the latest society and celebrity gossip.

←《

Mimi wasn't fond of another portrait that Maria de Kammerer painted of her, so she had it cut down. Her image was cropped out, but Boonie, the family dog, made it into the final frame. It rests alongside a twelve-foot-high black lacquer Chinese screen that belonged to her last husband's family.

》→

Family photos fill the table-tops and shelves of the bookcases in the library.

LIFE

A SURGEON DEPLORES
BLIND FEAR OF CANCER

NEW ELEGANCE IS ADDED
TO U.S. SOCIAL SCENE

MRS. AVERELL CLARK JR.
GOING TO SEATTLE PARTY

←《←《

Mimi and her second husband, Avy, each graced the cover of *Life* magazine, he on the November 1, 1943, issue as a World War II flying ace, she on the October 31, 1955, issue for epitomizing the Seattle social scene at Symphoneve, the city's first major society gala. Photos of our father (left, in the red frame, and center, with the mustache), Avy, and our aunt Carey are propped in front in the bookcases in her library.

》→

Mimi keeps an oval brass bar cart stocked in the dining room near the kitchen. Her favorite cocktail is Mount Gay Rum, the old sailor staple from Barbados, mixed with grapefruit juice.

》→

A Maria de Kammerer portrait of Aunt Carey as a young girl in Old Westbury hangs over the living room sofa.

←—≪

Equestrian art from Avy's family hangs on the padded celadon-and-ivory silk walls of the library.

≫—→

A small statue of one of Avy's family's horses that raced for them in France stands over the desk.

←«

Mimi's love of symmetry is evident all over the apartment, such as it is here, on the mantle in the library. Our aunt Carey admits that, as a child, she would often try to disturb one of her mother's many pairs of objects by hiding one of the pieces. It would always be back in place, mirroring its mate, by the time she returned to the scene of her mischievousness.

←«

Mimi also has a wonderful ability to mix high and low. Here she incorporates paper hydrangeas with crystal and an elaborate Venetian mirror.

CHRISTOPHER CLARK

Mimi's second husband, Avy Clark, and many of the men in his family flew planes and fought for the Allies. Like his uncle, Tommy Hitchcock, Jr., the young pilot hero of World War I who would become the greatest polo player in the world when he returned home to Old Westbury, Avy reached the rank of lieutenant colonel in the U.S. Army Air Forces. By the end of the Second World War, he had shot down sixteen Luftwaffe planes, dined with Eisenhower, and met Lady Bridget Elliot-Murray-Kynynmound, the striking brunette daughter of the 5th Earl of Minto. They married on April 19, 1944.

Lady Bridget spent her twenties running with the social elite of England and Scotland, drinking, skiing, hunting, and riding on some of Britain's greatest and most beautiful properties. After the war, she traded in her life of British aristocracy for that of American high society, and moved to Long Island with her new husband. In November 1949 in Southampton, New York, she gave birth to the couple's only child, Christopher. Christopher spent his early years in Florida and Old Westbury, but the family moved back to England when he was just three and his parents divorced two years later. Avy went back to the States, where he met and fell in love with our grandmother.

Shortly after the divorce, Lady Bridget remarried and they lived in a series of impressive homes in England and Scotland that epitomized the "English country house" style. Bridget collaborated with the famed decorators Nancy Lancaster and John Fowler, who, along with Sibyl Colefax, revolutionized the decor associated with country living, imbuing the once-austere interiors with elegance, color, and comfort. She had an innate eye and taste. In the 1960s, she partnered with a friend and a young protégée of Colefax and Fowler, Nina Campbell, to form their own decorating business, Elliot & Campbell. (After three years, Campbell went out on her own and is considered one of the top decorators in the world today.)

After growing up in homes that exuded the stylistic ideal of the region and era, Christopher found himself fascinated with the furniture that filled these manors and mansions. In his early twenties, he landed a spot in Sotheby's Institute of Art's Works of Art course. "Nine of us learned languages and style and how to go around the world looking at antiques," he said. After joining his stepbrothers (our dad and Uncle Peter) in Bolivia to tend to Avy's gold mine for a few years, he came back through New York and stopped by the Armory Antiques Show where he spotted a painting of four horses undergoing the very intimate gelding grooming process. He convinced Mimi to buy it and encouraged her to display it with pride (she did; it currently hangs in the seating area in her foyer), and simultaneously convinced the dealer, Mallett Antiques, to give him a job. Mallett, the venerable British firm, had opened up shop inside Bergdorf Goodman. So Christopher went to work selling antiques on the second floor, in between the fur department and the lingerie. But he increasingly spent more and more time up on the eleventh floor refurbishing Mallett's new acquisitions and quickly took over the firm's restoration department.

By 1977, Christopher decided it was time to head home to Scotland where he opened a small antiques shop of his own. With exchange rates in his favor, he started shipping antiques over from America, but then the dollar crashed and the plan went bust after three years. He was thirty years old and totally broke. He closed

the store and moved to London with a new plan: to make his own furniture—original designs and replicas of some of England's most famous pieces. He found a postage-stamp-sized spot to rent for five pounds a week in Shoreditch, at the time a rough, industrial part of London, and started his new venture.

"I didn't have any money at all. I slept on the floor. And I built it up from nothing," he remembers. The customers started to come—slowly. And then a small photo of the workshop landed on the pages of *Vogue Paris*. "Customers were coming in chauffer-driven cars," he said. "What a scene it was when the Duchess of Devonshire had to squeeze through the tiny newsstand in the front of the building to get back to my ten-by-fifteen-foot room. But my business snowballed after that."

He's continued that work ever since, these days from a workshop in Downham Market near his home in England's Norfolk region. He and his wife, Alice, an expert in decorative painting and trompe l'oeil murals, found an old Georgian farmhouse in shambles twenty years ago. They gutted the structure, maintaining the symmetrical eighteenth-century brick shell, and built an extremely cozy home for their three children, Thomas, Scarlett, and Jamie.

Wellington boots, oil paintings of the hunt, and photos of his family's property back in Scotland greet visitors when they enter through the mudroom. Alice painted the walls to look like creamy stone, and Berber carpet and Oriental rugs lie under toe. The main living room boasts yellow walls and chintz fabrics and is layered with Oriental rugs and oversize upholstered couches and walls of oil paintings depicting landscapes, hunting fare, and family, all surrounding a massive marble fireplace. Sun shines throughout, thanks to windows on both sides of the room—the front overlooks a gigantic magnolia and groomed bushes, and the back looks out onto a manicured lawn and a separate building that holds Alice's painting studio and the family billiards room.

In the adjoining dining room, a triptych depicting the Clark and Hitchcock families' hunts in Old Westbury hangs behind the circular dining table that Christopher made. After Sunday roasts, visitors can collapse onto the chairs and plush sofa by the other fireplace across from the dining room table. The bathrooms and the hallways are stacked, salon style, with photos and paintings of the family, including many of Tommy Hitchcock on horseback and Avy in his full pilot kit. Even though Christopher spent the majority of his life with the British side of the family, the Americans have a huge presence on the walls of this old farmhouse. However, there's not one crevice of this home where it's possible to forget that this is the English countryside. It's colorful, welcoming, and—above all— comfortable. Christopher and Alice's artistic talents are ingrained in practically all aspects of the home, punctuating the "English country house" style he learned from his mother and the world's most pre-eminent visionaries of English decor.

"The house was really just a shell when we bought it," Christopher said. "Everything's come from nothing really. Sometimes we were given things, sometimes we bought things, some of the things we made. Our home is a conglomeration of what we love."

←⊰←⊰←⊰

Christopher and Alice Clark
found this old Georgian
farmhouse in Norfolk,
England over twenty years
ago and gutted the struc-
ture, maintaining the symmetrical eighteenth-century
brick shell. Wellington boots,
oil paintings of hunting
expeditions, and photos of
his family's property back in
Scotland greet visitors when
they enter through the mudroom. Alice painted the walls
to look like creamy stone.

←⊰←⊰

The circa-1720 Fleur de
Pêche marble fireplace
was the most expensive
thing Christopher had ever
purchased and it became
the starting point of the
house's rebirth as it con-
ditioned the proportions
of the five doors that they
cut through the house. He
worried that it would be
too tall for the room, but
they uncovered a second,
higher ceiling from the old
hay loft and it fit perfectly.

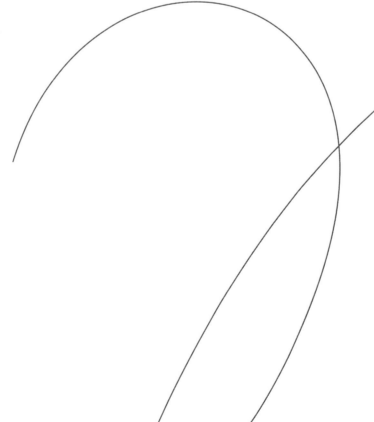

← ⫷

Family photos of Avy,
Christopher, Alice, and
their children, Thomas,
Scarlett, and Jamie, mingle
with important heirlooms
like the boxed saber given
to Christopher's mother
by Edith Roosevelt, Teddy
Roosevelt's wife.

⫸ →

A twenty-foot chimney col-
lapsed into the spare room
of Alice's mother's house
during the Great Storm of
1987 that killed more than
twenty people in England
and France. Guests were
due to stay in that room, but
luckily, they were delayed.
This Georgian mirror was
damaged severely during the
collapse, but Christopher
completely restored it to its
original state, and it now sits
on Alice's dressing table.

←‹‹←‹‹

Christopher's mother collaborated with the famed English-country-house-style decorators Nancy Lancaster, John Fowler, and Nina Campbell throughout her life. She gave Christopher the Chinese chess table in the foreground as a present for his eighteenth birthday. He later gave it to a cousin in lieu of rent. The cousin kindly restored it and gave it back when she came to stay with him twenty-odd years later.

››→

The guest bath near the entry serves as an homage to family with photos, sketches, and paintings hung salon-style up to the ceiling. The art includes portraits of Christopher's great-grandfather, the 4th Earl of Minto, who served as governor-general of Canada and governor-general of India; Alice's brother; Alice riding for the junior British team at the three-day European Eventing Championships in 1978; and her father, a great cricket champion. The cartoons they've collected over the years were drawn by friends and members of the family.

←‹‹

Family portraits of both the English and American sides of Christopher's family look out from the walls of the hallway on the first floor. A pastel sketch of Avy hangs across from a large photo of his uncle, Tommy Hitchcock, Jr., sitting on one of his polo ponies. Hitchcock played a key role in both world wars and died during a test flight of a P-51 Mustang fighter plane on the day of Avy and Bridget's wedding.

››→

An illustration of Alice's great-grandfather by the great British painter Charles "Snaffles" Johnson Payne hangs in the guest bathroom among the other family photos and sketches.

The Scottish Trifles.

Snaffles

The fox-hunt triptych that hangs in the Clark's dining room was part of a screen that used to stand in the Old Westbury, New York, home of Christopher's American, horse-loving grandmother, Helen Hitchcock. Painted by a Clark and Hitchcock family friend from Washington, D.C., the reverse side features wonderful chalk caricatures of all the key people in the painting.

CAREY CLARK

←◀◀←◀◀
A large portrait of Carey's father in his fighter pilot gear painted by Sir Oswald Birley in 1944 rests on bookshelves that hold her collection of family albums dating back to the dawn of photography. Carey's friend Andrea Hegeman painted the fabrics on most of the pillows.

←◀◀
An eighteenth-century portrait of Carey's great-great-great-great-uncle Valérien Allain from Louisiana, looks over her bedroom dresser. His great-granddaughter, Louise, married the great horse breeder and polo champion, Thomas Hitchcock, Sr., the father of Carey and Christopher's great uncle, Tommy Hitchcock, Jr.

Unlike most Midwesterners who flee to New York, I had a comfort zone waiting for me when I moved into my miniature one-bedroom on 85th Street and Third Avenue the week after college graduation. Mimi also lived on the Upper East Side (albeit more than a dozen blocks south and two monumentally fancier avenues west) and Aunt Carey was nearly two decades into her rent-controlled-by-handshake occupation of a full floor above Bubby's, a haven for comfort food and celebrity sightings in Tribeca. My family, it seemed to me, was living on two very different movie sets, the kinds of places that seemed too beautiful, too big, and far too "New York" to be real, especially compared to my Manhattan existence, which was encapsulated into 300 square feet in the midst of an area boasting two Barnes & Noble stores, three movie theaters, and about 1,235 bars that filled nightly with fraternity guys who wore square-toed, rubber-soled shoes with their suits and refused to tuck in their button-down shirts.

Where visits to Mimi's involved good posture, lamb, and bottomless glasses of wine, Carey's was all bohemian ease, farmers market salads, and even more bottomless glasses of wine with her scores of artist friends and collaborators. She used the front of the loft that looked over Hudson Street as a frame shop and artist studio and lived in the back. Books and papers and art projects covered an entire wall, while Oriental rugs lay on the high-gloss white painted cement floor, and the furniture—once quite grand, but a little tattered over the years—made it seem appropriate for everyone who came in to lie right down.

Then there was her bedroom. A blue-and-tan rug needlepointed by her paternal grandmother depicting leopards and antelope and elephants was sprawled across the floor; a large, dark, formal portrait of her great-great-great-great-uncle Valérien Allain from New Orleans hovered over the exposed brick wall at the head of her bed; and a silk screen by her friend Roy Lichtenstein of classical Greek columns and a tiny sea gull hung catty-corner to the portrait.

She lived in that Tribeca apartment for twenty-seven years, but five years ago, her rent went out of control and she had to leave. While she painted professionally for years and still runs her framing business, she'd also spent two decades volunteering and then working at the Point, an arts-based community center in the Hunts Point section of the South Bronx. The commute from the southwestern tip of Manhattan to the Bronx had been a burden anyway, so she sought out a new loft closer to work.

She moved to a new loft in an old, renovated mill building in the South Bronx, with original wood floors throughout and walls accented by exposed twelve-by-twelve-inch support beams that sits not far from Yankee Stadium. Her frame shop now has its own commercial space on the ground floor of the building, but there's ample room for painting off the dining area in her new loft. A large portrait of her father in his fighter pilot kit rests on bookshelves behind her gray angular upholstered couch and an acrylic coffee table. Her bedroom still has the portrait and the Lichtenstein silk screen, and many of her clothes hang inside the monogrammed Louis Vuitton steamer trunk that her needlepoint-loving grandmother, Helen Hitchcock, took around the world. Her bed sits on the gigantic antelope-print wool rug that once covered the floor of Mimi's apartment, where our mom and dad celebrated their wedding.

Though Carey now lives north of Mimi, her style will always be "downtown," and a world away from her mom's—even if many of the pieces in her current loft once resided on the Upper East Side. "Mum spent her life visiting her children's houses, moving their furniture," Carey said. "I think she loves it here, but she always seems to want to fix it up a bit. She says I can't put an African cloth on an old swivel chair and always asks when I'm going to get the place in shape. She wants to make it into the *House & Garden* aesthetic to which she ascribes—and I always work to curb her enthusiasm. It's quite a charming battle."

←—«

Carey's desk holds a collection of her favorite photos of family and friends, including her great-grandmother, Louise Eustis, on a fox hunt; her mom and dad; and the family's great friend, Eddie Morgan, the father of one of Carey's lifelong confidants, Alida Morgan. Carey painted the watercolor at the center, which depicts a dear friend standing in the Plaza de Toros in Ronda, Spain.

»—→

Carey's maternal grandmother (and our great-grandmother), Armenouhie Tashjian painted the flower still life that hangs on the northern wall of her space. She was the first female medical illustrator in the United States. Carey has painted for most of her adult life and still dedicates much of her loft to studio space, where she creates new work.

»—→

Carey's good friend, the pop artist Roy Lichtenstein, gave her the silk-screen print that hangs over her bed, between two Louise Lawler photos of Lichtenstein's work. The Russian brass nightstand belonged to Carey's grandmother, Helen Hitchcock.

»→

Carey fondly remembers visiting the Upper East Side apartment of her grandmother, Helen Hitchcock, and the ten-panel screen painted with French soldiers. Today, two of the panels— one of a chevalier, the other of an Algerian Zouave, and each with the seal of Paris painted on the back—help cordon off her dressing area.

»→

Many of Carey's clothes hang inside the monogrammed Louis Vuitton steamer trunk that her grandmother took around the world.

ALIDA MORGAN

It was 1975 and Diana Vreeland thought it was about time that Alida Morgan, a former protégée, meet her great-grandmother. Mrs. Vreeland, the legendary *Vogue* and *Harper's Bazaar* editor, was organizing the Metropolitan Museum's Costume Institute's American Women of Style exhibition, which highlighted ten of the most stylish women of the previous century, including Alida's great-grandmother, the art patron and artist, Gertrude Vanderbilt Whitney. So Mrs. Vreeland invited Alida to lunch, as she often did, and asked her to model her great-grandmother's outfits. "There I was, in her clothes, generations later," Alida said. "I never actually knew her, so it was a pretty wonderful way to sort of meet my great-grandmother."

Alida, a striking beauty with thick, pin-straight, long white hair, crystal-blue eyes, a voice kissed with smoke, and the continental accent one associates mainly with George Plimpton, may have walked in her great-grandmother's clothes briefly, but she lives with vestiges of her entire family and closest friends throughout the two floors she occupies in a Spanish Harlem townhouse filled with Victorian and Edwardian architectural features, elaborate plaster work, and Portuguese tile. Her heirlooms—which are interspersed with the furniture she decoratively painted back in the 1990s and her oversize paintings of flowers and sketches of manicured gardens for her new landscape design business—tell the story of her family's layered and often complicated past and the life she lived among artists, intellectuals, and decades-old confidants.

Alida's parents met after the war in Old Westbury. Her father's great-grandfather, Edwin Dennison Morgan, the twenty-first governor of New York and a one-term U.S. senator, bought up a series of Quaker farms in central Long Island during the middle of the nineteenth century. He sold large plots of the land to his friends, including the Whitney family. By the turn of the century, the Whitneys' property sat next to the Morgans', but each was so large that, as Alida's mother would later recall, "it took all day to ride the farm." So, it wasn't until after World War II that Nancy Marie Whitney met her longtime neighbor, a tall, dark, handsome U.S. Marine Corps hero of Guadalcanal, Edwin D. Morgan IV. "Daddy was so handsome and brooding. When he met Mum they fell madly in love," Alida said. "They proceeded to live together publicly—which was absolutely not done in their day."

Eddie and Nancy eventually decided to make things official. The wedding was planned, invitations sent. As the crowd of American high society gathered at the private chapel at Arden, the upstate New York estate that belonged to her stepfather, Averell Harriman, cold feet hit Nancy. "My grandmother said to her, 'You've been living together publicly for four years. You're not backing out now!'" So, she reluctantly went down the aisle and became Mrs. Morgan. With Averell Harriman running the Marshall Plan in Europe, the newlyweds headed to Paris. Eddie took his GI Bill at the Sorbonne at night and spent his days working at the Marshall Plan, helping rebuild the European economies in the face of Communism. Shortly thereafter, Alida, and then her sister, Pam, were born. In the end, however, her mother's wedding-day jitters proved true. Nancy and Eddie split when Alida was only three.

Eddie stayed in Paris to make a life in business while socializing with and befriending many of the literary elite of postwar Europe. When his friend George Plimpton wanted to start a new

literary journal in the early 1950s, Eddie gave him space in his office; *The Paris Review* was born. He eventually moved back to the States and became one of our grandmother's most loyal, treasured friends for over three decades.

Meanwhile, Alida and her sister Pam moved to Princeton with their mother after a stop in Sun Valley for the divorce, and then to the Whitney family compound in the Adirondacks. Their mother married a beau of her cousin Gloria Vanderbilt and took the family to Mexico for a couple years. When that broke up, they headed for Chicago and a third marriage to her second husband's brother. That relationship, too, ended. When Alida was a senior at Foxcroft School in Virginia, ready to head off to college, her mother suddenly announced that she was returning to Paris. Alida changed her plans and said she'd enroll at the Sorbonne so she could be with the family.

"All our stuff is on the boat for France. The monkey has been given to the Brookfield Zoo, the dogs have passports," she recalled. "We're gathered at my grandmother's house on 81st Street, but my mother was nowhere to be found. Then the phone rang." It was her mother, calling to report "strange and wonderful" news. "That's how we found out that she was marrying our last stepfather, Pierre," Alida said. Instead of Paris, Alida ended up at Finch College, then Georgetown then Yale, where she was part of the first class of women transfer students, and where she is further distinguished as the first woman to be kicked out.

After Yale and a short stint modeling, her roommate, Nicky Vreeland, told his grandmother that Alida needed to do something more rewarding. So, Mrs. Vreeland asked Alida come work for her at the Costume Institute. Her work with Mrs. Vreeland led to a job as sittings editor at *Harper's Bazaar* where she met a series of dynamic women with whom she forged incredibly enduring friendships that thrive to this day.

After such a peripatetic youth, home has become a very special thing to Alida. "Because Mummy got married and moved so much, we always spent every summer in Long Island with my grandparents, and up with the cousins in the Adirondacks," Alida explained. "We used the New York house as our sort of touchstone. New York was always, in a way, home base, even though we were living in other places."

Today, her two floors in Spanish Harlem are her true home base, filled with representations of family and friends who lived all over. Her father and grandfather are there, looking out over her living room in a grand portrait painted by a cousin and notable portrait artist, Lydia Field Emmet. Her great-grandmother Gertrude, her sister, her step-siblings, her friends and mother, Cousin Gloria and all the husbands hang around in photos on all the walls. There is a mismatched escritoire and bookcase that her grandmother, Marie Norton Harriman, bought in France on her honeymoon with Cornelius Vanderbilt Whitney. At night, Alida rests her head against her great-grandmother Beulah's headboard that belonged to a Portuguese sea captain almost four hundred years ago. After a life of constant movement, Alida, at 62, has shored up her experiences and settled down in a home that reflects all the houses and places, people, and things she's ever loved.

←⫷ ←⫷ ←⫷
The two floors that Alida occupies in a Spanish Harlem townhouse are filled with representations of family and friends who have lived all over the world, providing her a home base full of memories and personalities after a life of frenetic movement.

←⫷ ←⫷
A large painting by her cousin, the notable portrait artist Lydia Field Emmet, of her father and grandfather, looks out over her living room, next to a smaller portrait of her maternal grandmother, Marie Norton Harriman.

←⫷
Alida's mother, Nancy Marie Whitney, and her fourth husband, Pierre Lutz, bought the two-hundred-year-old kilim rug from the Jacques Carcanagues Gallery in Soho for their house in Redding, Connecticut. Pierre, an architect, favored a crisp, modern, "white on white" decor punctuated by a few well-chosen antiques. Nancy was bohemian and loved color and the dramatic, but they both agreed on that rug.

←⫷
Alida's grandmother bought the mismatched escritoire and bookcase in France on her honeymoon with her first husband, Cornelius Vanderbilt Whitney. It sat in the living room in her house on Hobe Sound, Florida where she brought her second husband, Averell Harriman, to fish, play croquet and cards, and entertain. After Averell died, the piece fell into the hands of Pamela Harriman, his wartime mistress who later became his wife. Alida reclaimed it at auction following Pamela's death.

←—«

The Napoleonic child's chair in her living room belonged to her uncle, Harry Whitney, and resided in the New York apartment of Alida's maternal grandmother, Marie Norton Harriman, and her second husband, Averell Harriman.

←—«

When she lived in San Francisco in the 1990s, Alida began customizing old pieces of furniture with her own hand-painted patterns, including this highboy dresser that graces the corner of her bedroom beneath a print of the Alida, a mid-nineteenth-century Hudson River steamboat, a gift from her friend Sophie Engelhard Craighead. Friends and family have given her prints of the Alida steamboat throughout her life.

← «

During the Art Deco craze of the 1920s, many well-to-do families on New York's Upper East Side stripped their homes of their Edwardian and Victorian interiors. To be closer to their clients, many contractors overseeing the projects moved to East Harlem, including the man who bought the townhouse where Alida now lives. He added in plasterwork, soaring arched doorways, etched glass slipper doors, and other architectural elements salvaged from his projects on the Upper East Side to create a beautiful, yet period-unspecific interior to the building.

» →

Alida's mother married three times before meeting her last husband, Pierre, at her cousin's camp in the Adirondacks. The two were engaged after four days and remained married for the remainder of Pierre's life. Pierre painted the watercolor of Alida that hangs in her upstairs bathroom.

»→
When not being used for her frequent dinner parties, the dining room serves double duty as a studio where Alida makes her oversize paintings of flowers and designs manicured gardens for her new landscape design business.

»→
Alida's mother found this dresser at a junk store in New York in the 1950s.

← ⋘

Alida rests her head against her great-grand-mother Beulah's head-board, which originally belonged to a Portuguese sea captain almost four hundred years ago.

⋙ →

Alida's paternal grandmother and her father both loved and collected Bristol blue glass from the eighteenth and nineteenth centuries. Alida has carried on the tradition and mixes the old pieces from her family with modern designs either hand-blown by her stepbrother, Antoine Lutz, or given to her by friends. Much of her collection has broken over the years, but she believes that "one should use pretty things, not harbor them, so loss is less of a big deal."

ALEXA ROMANOFF

The woman born Princess Alexandra Pavlovna Galitzine received a tremendous gift on her seventy-eighth birthday: her second granddaughter. To commemorate the day, remarkable on many levels, her son and his wife gave their new baby girl her name. The two Alexandras—the older, known to friends and family as "Aleka" Armour; the younger, "Alexa" Romanoff—became kindred spirits and confidantes until Armour's death at 101 in 2006.

Alexa vividly remembers all the times she slipped away with her grandmother to the wood-paneled study of her stately home in Lake Forest, Illinois. "At night, I'd go sit with her as she had her last cigarette. I can still remember the smell—it was that cedar, tobacco, perfume mix," she recalls.

When Alexa was two, her father got a job in London and the family moved across the ocean. But the Alexandras' ritual of retreat to that office and other rooms in the house continued throughout her entire childhood on visits back to the Midwest. She remembers struggling to turn off two of her grandmother's lamps carved in the shape of Crimean War soldiers because the switches were different from those she knew back in England. "My grandmother would always retire to that office after breakfast, in her dressing gown, and open her mail by these two lamps," Alexa said. Today, those soldiers stand guard on either side of a sofa from her mother's childhood home in Rockford, Illinois, within the pale lavender living room of her sunny duplex in London's West Kensington neighborhood.

Alexa also spent hours at her grandmother's side, watching as she carefully stitched wool yarns through canvas to create needlepoint swatches for furniture and pillows that she always loved to give as treasured presents. For Alexa's christening, Aleka needlepointed an image of Jean de Brunhoff's Babar and Celeste on their wedding day as a seat cover for Alexa's baby chair. It sits at the end of Alexa's entry hall today.

Another one of Aleka's creations—a beautiful floral-patterned Louis XVI bench—stands in front of the French doors that lead to her tiny back garden off her bedroom on the ground floor. "This piece is particularly special as it was the last piece that she completed before she died," Alexa said. "She said needlepointing kept her eyesight in pretty good nick. I love it because it was something that she was dedicated to and although it is not her finest piece, I adore it for the imperfections and the memories."

It's a feat for anyone to live past one hundred, but even more so for Armour. Her father was grand marshal of the nobility of the province of Novgorod and a member of the Council of State for the royal court of Czar Nicholas II. After the assassination of the czar, his wife, and children during the Russian Revolution, Aleka's family failed to escape Russia. She and her brother, Nicholas, were separated from their five other siblings and sent to a Soviet prison. Three years later, Aleka and Nick managed to flee, making it to Hungary and then England. When traveling through Budapest on the Russian Orthodox Easter during their escape, Aleka thought her pious mother would be upset if they skipped their Easter prayers, even though neither of them had seen their siblings or parents since the separation. She convinced Nick to duck into a random church and pray. They looked up into the choir and saw their sister. This story was one of the few details Aleka ever mentioned to her granddaughter about her persecution and escape.

In London, Aleka met the man who became her first husband, Prince Rostislav Alexandrovich Romanoff, the son of Grand Duke Alexander Mikhailovich and Grand Duchess Xenia Alexandrovna, Czar Nicholas II's older sister. Completely besotted, he followed her across the globe to Chicago, where she had moved to help Nick perfect his English for his new position at Commonwealth Edison. They divorced, and in 1949, she married Lester Armour, a president of the Harris Bank of Chicago and grandson of the founder of the Armour meat-packing company.

Alexa's parents met in Lake Forest, not far from where her mother, Christia Anne Ipsen, had grown up. When it came to her children, Christia made an effort to weave the rich history of their father's Russian family in with her own special traditions. "One year at Christmas, my mom decided that instead of giving us toys and material things we would lose or grow out of, she would give antiques, prints, and objects that we would use later in life," Alexa said. The equestrian print that hangs over her dresser was one of the first of these keepsake gifts. "I have always been fascinated with horses and grew up with them. However, I remember being a little bit confused when this tradition started, as I am sure that I asked for something like a CD player," she said.

Alexa's mother made antiquing and vintage shopping a year-round activity for her children—and always seemed to slip it into their daily routines. "We'd go out for groceries and come home with old blankets and apple crates," Alexa remembers. When she hit her teens, Alexa began to seek out her own old keepsakes. On a trip to the large Ardingly Antiques Fair in southern England, she splurged on a pair of big yellow lamps, her first substantial purchase. One broke years ago, but the survivor sits on the dresser in her bedroom, next to that horse print her mom had bought her for Christmas when she was young.

Like her mother-in-law, Christia also loves needlework. It was she who stitched the Romanoff coat of arms and its double-headed eagle onto a canvas during one of the family trips to Nantucket. The resulting velvet-backed pillow sits on a red leather club chair in Alexa's living room. Those sixty-four square inches of looped wool represent the heavy legacy of Alexa's father's family—and the traditions and crafts of the two women who've been closest to Alexa her whole life.

←⫷ ←⫷

Alexa Romanoff has filled her sunny duplex in London's South Kensington neighborhood with heirlooms from her paternal grandmother and the antiques that her mother has given her for Christmas every year since she was a preteen.

←⫷

Throughout her childhood, Alexa loved watching her Russian grandmother, Aleka, open her mail by a pair Crimean War soldier lamps in the office of her Lake Forest, Illinois, home. This one and its mate sit on either side of Alexa's living room sofa today.

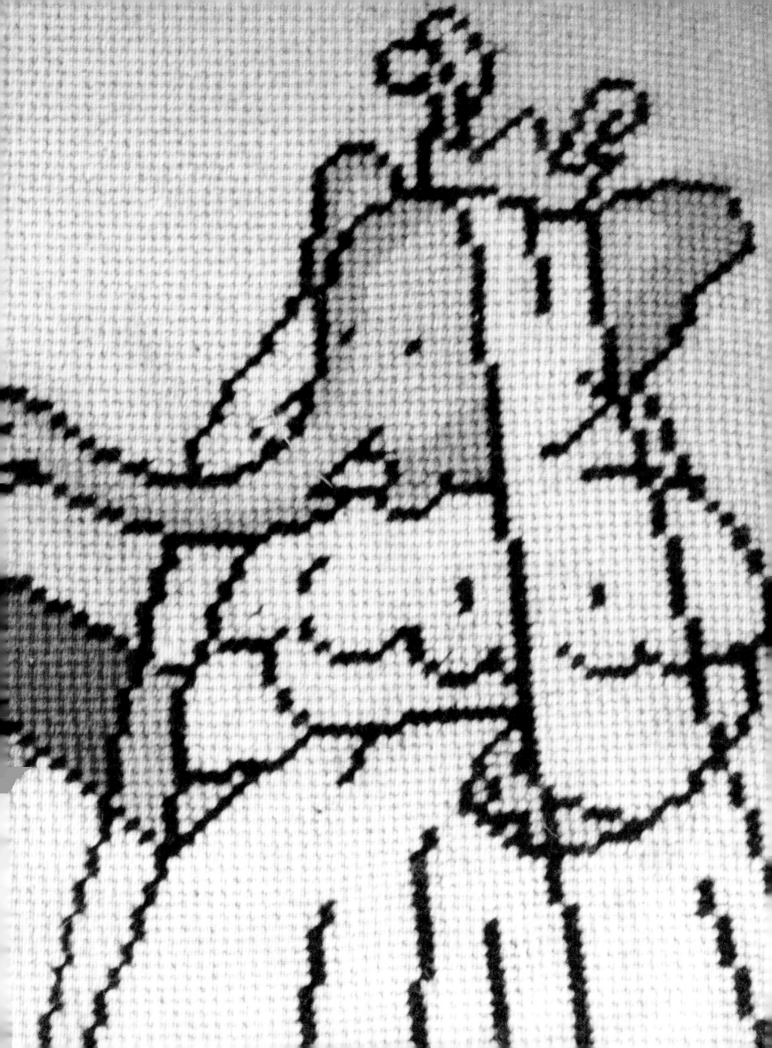

←‹‹‹ ←‹‹‹
For Alexa's christening,
Aleka, an avid needlepointer,
stitched Jean de Brunhoff's
beloved royal elephants,
Babar and Celeste, on their
wedding day, to cover the
seat of Alexa's baby chair.
It sits at the end of Alexa's
entryway hall today.

←‹‹‹
This bench was Aleka's final
needlepoint project before
she died at 101. Alexa cher-
ishes it for the imperfections.

←—«

On a trip to the large
Ardingly Antiques Fair in
southern England, Alexa
splurged on a pair of big
yellow lamps, her first
substantial purchase. One
broke years ago, but the
survivor sits on the dresser
in her bedroom, next to
the horse print her mom
bought her for Christmas
when she was young.

»—→

Alexa has sprinkled references to the Romanoff
family throughout her flat.
Her mother commissioned
the bracelet featuring the
family's coat of arms.

Alexa and her mother found this red leather club chair at a Brooklyn flea market. The painting that hangs over the mantel is by her older brother, who now lives in Russia.

Alexa's mother, Christia, also loves needlework. Christia stitched the Romanoff coat of arms and its double-headed eagle onto a canvas during one of the family's trips to Nantucket.

SEAN CROWLEY

At Cornelius F. Dunn Middle School in Danvers, Massachusetts, Sean Crowley's eighth grade teacher was a true Anglophile. He taught his students the difference between a "lorry" and a "truck"; the historical details of the Titanic disaster as part of a lesson on *A Night to Remember* that extended half the year; and that everyone will do better on a test if they throw on a shirt and tie. And he told his class that anyone who dressed up on exam day would receive extra credit.

"It was a significant amount of points—I think around ten. Quite a bump," Sean said. "So of course I was going to do it. But I thought, hey, let's take this all the way."

As a boy, he spent hours at his maternal grandparents' house next door watching classic British shows like *Upstairs, Downstairs* and *Are You Being Served?* as his grandfather, John Burbidge, the long-time head designer at Boston's beloved bridal shop, Priscilla's of Boston, stitched and sewed next to him. Young Sean soon became enamored of *Jeeves & Wooster*, the wonderful, early 1990s TV adaptation of the P. G. Wodehouse stories starring Hugh Laurie and Stephen Fry.

He realized that the 1930s white tie and tails his grandfather wore when he took his wife Cile waltzing at the Harvard Club looked an awful lot like the ones worn by Jeeves—and he loved it.

So when test day came, Sean borrowed his grandfather's full kit—right down to the detached collar and patent oxfords— and hit the halls of middle school like he was rolling to the opera in 1932. He got his bonus points, as well as an enduring taste for Edwardian formalwear.

"A lot of people asked, 'What the hell are you doing?' My classmates found it amusing and I loved getting a laugh as much as I actually loved the clothes," Sean recalls. "It served two purposes—and amazingly no one beat me up."

Given his love of costume and inspiring a crowd, Sean always thought he'd be involved in theater or movies. He landed at film school at Emerson College in Boston, but gave up that path after a semester in Los Angeles. Instead, he followed his love of the old, and after graduating, sold college scarves, vintage J. Press tweeds, and Brooks Brothers blazers at Bobby from Boston, the notable South End vintage shop.

He eventually landed on the sales floor of the Ralph Lauren store on Newbury Street and then in the company's flagship in the Rhinelander Mansion, on 72nd and Madison Avenue in New York. He so looked the part of an early-twentieth-century WASP that on one stroll through the store, Ralph noticed him and offered him a job in the design department.

Outside of Buckingham Palace, there may be no place greater for a curious American Anglophile to spend his days than Ralph Lauren's headquarters. Sean's job as a neckwear designer there for the past six years has given him ample new opportunities—and justification—to keep up his collecting, which has expanded past clothing into every kind of curio produced with care in England, continental Europe, or the Northeastern United States at the turn of the last century.

Heraldic plaques and roe antlers frame the mirror above the marble mantelpiece in the living room of the apartment he shares with his girlfriend, Meredith Modzelewski, on the third floor of a beautiful Fort Greene, Brooklyn, brownstone. They face a triptych

of three-dimensional wood and ceramic Chinoiserie panels that his grandfather John made decades ago and his uncle's 1920s rattan couch for which his mom made slipcovers. Heaps of regimental helmets sit in an armchair in the corner, next to portraits of British gentry and royals. Hundreds of crystal decanters and bottles of brown liquor flow across the top of an old Victrola right onto the floor.

Then there's the closet and much of his bedroom where he keeps all of his clothing, a result of over fifteen years of flea-market shopping. He has over three thousand ties, hundreds of jackets and blazers, and stacks of schoolboy scarves that reach multiple feet to the ceiling. Frankly, Sean could practically outfit an entire boarding school—and much of the Queen's army—with what he has on hand.

Even with the abundance of treasures, he makes a concerted effort to integrate most of his collections and the individual pieces in them into his daily life. He wears the beautiful old clothes, shakes out cocktails from that overflowing bar, and serves his tea from an old English teapot. For parties, he entertains with authentic Victorian customs. He serves trifle and puts fruit-laden ice ring sculptures into his elaborate punches. And most importantly, he investigates and appreciates the stories behind every object or piece that he acquires, including the gifts his close family has handed down or made for him. Years ago, he came across a big ceremonial mug during a random eBay search. After it arrived, he poked around and discovered that the same artist had made this series of mugs for Wedgwood over the course of fifty years or more. Over thirty of them now hang in his kitchen.

When it comes to handing his collection over to the next generation, Sean hopes eventually to inspire some lucky Anglophile, just like his eighth grade teacher and grandfather did by sharing their passion with him. "Honestly, I'm sure that when the time came, I would love to pass my collection to a likeminded young lunatic who would love and appreciate it as much as I have."

←◀◀ ←◀◀

Sean's maternal grandparents, John and Cile, used to throw big, beautiful parties, but they weren't big drinkers, so they stored the bottles of spirits brought by guests in a cabinet behind a sofa. Sean liberated loads of these bottles for his extensive booze collection that pours onto his living room floor.

←◀◀

John and Cile's "gurgling cod" water pitchers make a gurgling sound when poured and pay homage to Boston's cod-fishing history. Sean displays them beneath a pencil portrait that his grandfather sketched of a friend from his unit in the mechanized infantry during World War II.

←‹‹

Sean's father and grandfather
John both collect hats as well;
however, unlike Sean, they
don't wear theirs. Many of
the hats in Sean's collection
that he found over the years
online and at flea markets
are pure costume and only
get worn for fancy dress parties, Halloween, or intimate,
cocktail-fueled dinner parties.

››→

Sean pulled these umbrel-
las out of the trash and had
them re-covered by one of
Brooklyn's last "umbrella
men," who has perfected
the craft of umbrella repair.

←—«

The Fort Greene apartment that Sean shares with his girlfriend, Meredith Modzelewski, features prewar architectural details including a stately marble mantelpiece that holds many of Sean's flea market trinkets and family photos.

←—«

The three terra-cotta-on-wood panels by his grandfather John depict a Japanese poem. Sean's mother made many of the pillows out of embroidery panels that her mother had stitched throughout the years.

»—→

A photo of Sean's grandparents on a date during their college years in the 1940s sits on the mantel. His grandfather dons a perfectly draped double-breasted Glen plaid suit, and Cile is decked out in a black gown trimmed with ermine tails that she made.

Sean splits his enormous collection of vintage clothing between an office and his bedroom. The office (pictured here) holds hundreds of tweed jackets and school blazers and an entire library of reference books on everything from eighteenth-century kitchen utensils to 1930s French pornography.

≫→

The silk lining of the gray topper (top row, center) is covered with signatures of friends and guests who partied with its previous owner across England and at the Ascot races in the 1930s.

≫→

Growing up, the Crowleys always had two or three of these letterpress-type trays on the walls, which Sean's father filled with all the "smalls" he found at the flea market. Sean has maintained the tradition, filling his with tiny curiosities and stoneware Wade Whimsies (like the pig on the upper left), figurines from tea boxes that his family collected.

ANGUS TRUMBLE

It was 1975 in Melbourne, Australia, when Manet, Monet, and Matisse came to town. From that point on, ten-year-old Angus Trumble knew he'd do something with art for the rest of his life.

"My interest in art was stimulated both by my parents, who were amateur painters, and the experience of having seen as a child one of the first large-scale blockbuster exhibitions ever to be brought to Australia, the Modern Masters show from the Museum of Modern Art in New York," he said. "That was an enormous event in Australia. I was interested in art from that point onward."

As a schoolboy, Angus painted and even flirted with the idea of going to art school, but went for art history instead, with dreams of someday working in a museum. In the mid-1990s, he came to New York for graduate school at the Institute of Fine Arts at New York University and then landed a job back home at the Art Gallery of South Australia in Adelaide. There, he had access to a very fine and large collection of Victorian British paintings, most of which the gallery acquired directly from the artists' studios in the nineteenth century.

"Since we had very modest resources, most of the exhibitions that we organized were drawn from the permanent collection," Angus said. "So I did a lot of shows over a relatively short span of years in the area of British art because that's what we had to work with."

Today, Angus is senior curator of paintings and sculpture at the Yale Center for British Art. There, he works with the museum's expansive collection, which includes oils depicting Britain's great naval battles, scores of canvases highlighting the best of British sporting life, and hundreds of other visiting and permanent works to hang inside Louis Kahn's calming, cement, postmodern 1969 architectural masterpiece on Yale's campus in New Haven, Connecticut.

For his personal collection that hangs on the walls of his redbrick arts-and-crafts Tudor just west of campus, Angus chooses key pieces from his favorite Australian painters and the artists he's known and befriended over the years since he lived in the United States.

A dark, oversize painting of mischievous boys struggling underwater by Yale MFA grad Maximilian Toth presides over the two-story entry, not far from two space-themed paintings by Angus's friend, Suzanne Treister, whom he met in Adelaide, pastel drawings from noted Australian artist David Harley, and a wonderful outsider art painting of three somewhat crudely rendered but charming bush birds.

"This is a wonderful treasure by an aboriginal painter called Patsy Lulpunda who lived the whole of her life in the Kimberley region of Western Australia," Angus says about the bird painting. "She turned one hundred in about 1998. In the British Commonwealth, if you turn one hundred, and someone alerts Buckingham Palace, you get a telegraph or a card from the Queen. She did, and it threw her into such a spasm of excitement that she took up painting. In the final eighteen months of her life, she produced about fifty pictures, mostly of these bush birds, and I just love them."

All four walls of his dining room are covered in uniformly framed, carefully arranged black-and-white family photos. There's Angus's great-grandmother's family on the day of her engagement, lounging on kangaroo-skin rugs; portraits of his grandfather as a small boy in a sailor outfit and then as a man in his World War I Royal Naval Air Service captain's uniform; and his grandmother on the day she was presented at court, decked in the obligatory two ostrich feathers, veil, and train with a massive bouquet. "Most of the photos came to light after my mother died, and had come into her possession as a consequence of spending half a lifetime looking after elderly relations," he said. "I always thought that old photographs make a good form of decoration for a dining room because they stimulate so many forms of conversation, particularly the more unconventional ones."

Ultimately, he'd like the family archive—papers and photos included—to go as a collection to the National Library of Australia, but for the time being they will continue to stay right with him. These pieces keep Australia alive in his home.

"On a very elementary level, it was really the cumulative gift of experiences with my Australian family that allowed me to follow my dreams and purchase this house in the first place," he said. "So I've felt the chorus of long-since-vanished relatives was largely responsible for propelling me here, and this is my homage to them."

←—«← —«
Angus, a renowned expert in British art, has filled his arts-and-crafts Tudor just west of the Yale University campus with pieces of art and family photos from Australia, his native country.

»»—→
Aboriginal painter Patsy Lulpunda started painting at the age of one hundred after receiving a birthday greeting from Queen Elizabeth II. In the final eighteen months of her life, she produced about fifty pictures, including the painting of the bush birds that hangs in Angus's entryway.

»⌐

Two space-themed paintings by Angus's friend Suzanne Treister, whom he met in Adelaide, hang near the passage to his expansive library.

»→

Most of Angus's books made a journey from Adelaide to Melbourne by truck, across the Pacific Ocean to Seattle by boat, and then back on a truck across the continental United States. The whole process took four months.

A portrait of Angus's great-great-great-great-grandmother, Jane Pearson, painted around 1820, hangs over the arts-and-crafts fireplace in his library. The painting arrived in Australia from her home in Scotland in the 1860s. It was around that time that the family placed the painting into this ornate frame, turning it into a composite colonial object.

Jane's son, Commander Hugh Pearson, was an officer in the Royal Navy during the Napoleonic Wars and fought the French on the northern coast of Spain. Miniature portraits of him during the Napoleonic era, and his great-granddaughter—Angus's maternal grandmother—during World War I sit on a side table in the library.

Romantic Realist

ELBULL
H·H·WALSH

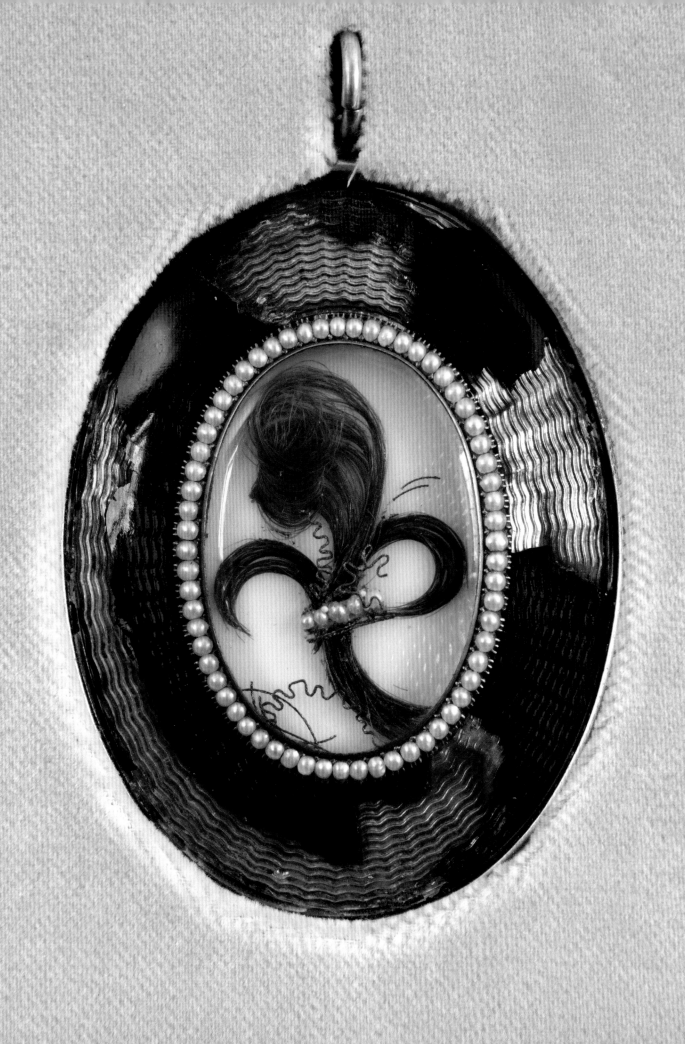

← ⫷← ⫷

A front and back view of the miniature portrait of Angus's great-great-great-grandfather in his Royal Navy uniform. A lock of his hair is encased in the back. After the Napoleonic Wars in 1815, he retired from the Navy and returned to Scotland to marry and eventually father fourteen children. After his death in 1838 or 1839, his oldest son, William, emigrated to Victoria, establishing the family line in Australia.

⫸→↑

When Angus's mother died, she left behind an enormous accumulation of old photographs, many of which hang salon-style over all four walls of his dining room, matted in matching wooden frames. "I always thought that old photographs make a good form of decoration for a dining room because they stimulate so many forms of conversation, particularly the more unconventional ones," he says.

⫸→

The images in the dining room include shots of Angus's great-grandmother's family on the day of her engagement, lounging on kangaroo-skin rugs; portraits of his grandfather in his World War I Royal Naval Air Service captain's uniform; and his grandmother on the day she was presented at court.

TREY SPEEGLE

When Trey Speegle bought his nineteenth-century barn in the Catskills as a weekend retreat and studio, he wanted every inch covered in white, save for the high-gloss black floors and the two-story chimney. It took a hundred gallons of gleaming alabaster to create this blank canvas. But once he added all the art and furniture created and given by his those closest to him over the past three decades, he managed to create a portrait of his life as an artist, designer, and loyal friend to many of the notable players of the art, publishing, and entertainment scenes in 1980s New York City.

"When you get a bit older, you know what the odds are, so if you don't think you can do something, you don't even try," he said. "I had no idea that I couldn't come to New York from Texas at age twenty and get a job at *Vogue*." But he did. He moved to the East Village during the height of the 1980s art boom, landed the assistant art editor position at *Vogue* and befriended artists like Keith Haring and Kenny Scharf and David McDermott and Peter McGough. "I had a dual life," he said. "Everyone else was a starving artist, and I was a starving Condé Nast employee."

In the late '80s, McDermott and McGough invited Trey to a Christmas party given by their friend, Michael O'Donoghue, Saturday Night Live's first head-writer. Trey knew O'Donoghue's work from SNL and *The National Lampoon* and wanted to impress, so he figured he'd better bring a memorable gift. His boyfriend at the time was friendly with Andy Warhol and had just received a Christmas gift from him, wrapped in white paper with Warhol's signature scrawled across it. "At Condé Nast that year, we got these doorknob-sized, cut crystal Tiffany paperweights for Christmas and for some reason I had two," he said. "So I took one, put it into its blue box with orange paper and wrapped it in the white 'Andy' paper and wrote: 'To Michael O'Donoghue, Merry Christmas! XX Trey Speegle and Andy Warhol.' That kooky gesture was the start of our friendship."

With a long list of mutual friends and both having a similar biting sense of humor, Trey and O'Donoghue became fast friends and collaborators. One day, O'Donoghue mentioned that he'd like to do something with the 250 paint-by-number paintings that he'd picked up at flea markets throughout the years. Trey suggested that they try to pitch a show highlighting the popularity and symbolism of these hobby kits. Cultural critics had viewed paint-by-number paintings as a symbol of the mindless conformity gripping 1950s America, but thousands of hobbyists catapulted the craft kits to iconic status and popularity. East Village gallery owner Paul Bridgewater loved the concept and put on the show to rave reviews.

O'Donoghue died suddenly from an aneurysm two years later at age fifty-four. Understanding their kinship and likeminded taste, his widow, Cheryl Hardwick, bequeathed the entire collection of paint-by-number paintings to Trey, along with a taxidermied baby alligator, the Gustav Stickley-designed Arts-and-Crafts wooden chair her husband sat in when he typed his jokes, and a gold baby grand piano that Hardwick had affectionately dubbed "Goldie." The gifts, which all reside in his farmhouse, proved bittersweet on two very different levels. Trey took the paint-by-numbers-as-a-cultural-icon concept to the Smithsonian, which, in turn, mounted a yearlong exhibition on the craft to coincide with the fortieth anniversary of these kits. As importantly, these paintings led to an artistic epiphany for Trey. He started to collect and use these craft works as a

medium for his own form of pop art, adding words and phrases to the designs to make social commentary with—and on top of—one of the twentieth century's most pervasive symbols of consumerism and mass culture. Over the last decade, he has amassed over three thousand of these paintings (some finished, some not) and made a successful art career using them in his own paintings and collages.

Trey cultivated countless other friendships over the years, based on similar generosity and shared aesthetic passion. The evidence of these relationships resides all over his barn. A McDermott and McGough portrait of a man with cut-out eyes and a Dagwood and Blondie painting by Suzanne Mallouk, the "Widow Basquiat," hang behind Goldie and the taxidermied alligator at the back of the barn. A Warhol cow, part of a set that Trey bought for himself and an ex, looks out over the living room area featuring an old wooden table from his close friend, Penny McCall, the 3M heiress, art patron, and philanthropist, who died in a tragic mountainside accident with her husband while on an aid mission in Albania in 1999.

The entire front wall of the barn serves as a memorial to others Trey loved and admired. In 1987 on a trip to Italy, McDermott and McGough discovered and brought back stacks of blank memorial posters that many Italian villages use to announce deaths. When Warhol died shortly after their return, Trey took one of the posters, added Warhol's name and high school yearbook photo, and plastered a thousand copies all over downtown Manhattan. In an ultimate spirit of found art, Warhol's brother gave one of the posters to the gravestone maker and it became the template for Warhol's eternal marker in Pittsburgh, now a place of pilgrimage for art lovers. The original poster is framed over the entry door next to a rubbing of Warhol's gravestone. Trey repeated this memorial a couple years later when Salvador Dalí passed and again when his dear friend, Juan Botas, the Spanish illustrator who inspired Jonathan Demme to make his film *Philadelphia*, died of AIDS.

In a trick he picked up from O'Donoghue, Trey keeps his wildest curiosities (a Tiger sneaker signed by Warhol, a paper plate he swiped from a picnic after a shoot with Justin Timberlake, a Victorian taxidermied cat, and a bounced check from Courtney Love-Cobain) inside a large freestanding glass display case on the right side of the massive open living area inside the barn. Everything inside that cabinet and the entire weekend retreat pays homage to the incredible lives, talents, and experiences of Trey and his group of friends. Fittingly, it's all displayed against a clean white background with a sense of irony and humor—just like the most evocative pieces of pop art.

←—«←—«

The entire front wall of Trey's barn serves as a memorial to artists, including Andy Warhol, Salvador Dalí, and his friend, Juan Botas, whose life and death from AIDS inspired the film *Philadelphia*.

←⫷←⫷←⫷

Trey has amassed one of the world's largest collections of paint-by-number paintings and craft kits after inheriting about two hundred fifty from his close friend Michael O'Donoghue. Trey now uses paint-by-number paintings as materials for his own paintings and collages. His friends David McDermott and Peter McGough painted the "Trusses and Toupes" piece on an old window.

←⫷←⫷

In a trick he picked up from O'Donoghue, Trey keeps his most wild curiosities inside a large glass display case, which stands on the right side of the massive open living area inside the barn.

⫸→

Andy Warhol was in New York signing objects and a friend of Trey's, the artist Mary Hayslip, brought in ten pairs of white go-go boots, the lid to her sewing machine, and this pair of white canvas sneakers. Warhol signed them all.

⫸→

Next to a bounced check from Courtney Love-Cobain sits a Mexican memorial photo composed of a carved, painted suit with a hand-tinted photo glued on as the head, all inside a handmade wooden frame. Trey found the baseball at Andy Warhol's grave in Pittsburgh and brought it home.

A McDermott and McGough portrait of a man with cut-out eyes looks out over Goldie, the gold baby grand piano that Michael O'Donoghue's widow, Cheryl Hardwick, gave to Trey after Michael died.

A David McDermott line drawing of Trey sits in the rafters on the second story of the barn.

DERMOT 63

TREY SPEEGLE

←—◀◀

Trey had admired McDermott and McGough's "Jesus Christ and Holy Mother Mary of God for Middle Collegiate Church, Easter Sunday, 1928" at an East Village show in the mid-1980s. The next day, they came to his apartment, painting in hand, and sold it to him—after some very easy bargaining—for forty dollars. The teacup comes from McDermott and McGough's San Francisco Earthquake series. Both pieces sit on an old wooden table from Trey's friend, Penny McCall, the art patron who died in a tragic mountainside accident in 1999.

▶▶—→

Goldie, the baby grand piano, fills the entire back right corner of the barn and is surrounded by art and objects from Trey's friends and artists like Keith Haring and Suzanne Mallouk. Trey's dog, Lamonte, rests on one of the paint-by-number-inspired rugs that Trey designed for Anthropologie.

Craftint BIG 3 SET
THE CRAFTINT MANUFACTURING CO. • CLEVELAND 10, OHIO
paint with numbered colors
SERIES D2
• ITALIAN WATERFRONT
• ITALIAN ALPS
• FISHING VILLAGE
SERIES P-1
• PARADISE COVE
• THE RICE PLANTERS
• HOME IN THE TROPIC
SERIES L3
• NOTRE DAME CATHEDRAL
• EIFFEL TOWER
• ARC DE TRIUMPH
easy

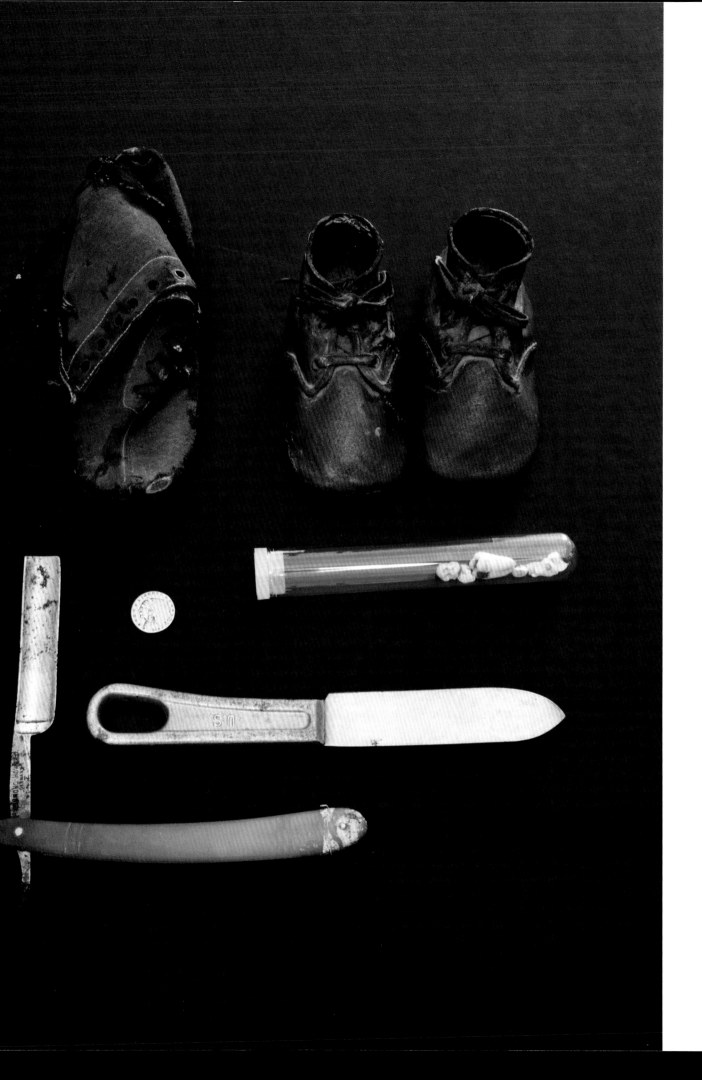

← ≪ ← ≪

Trey collects both finished paint-by-number paintings and original kits, which he keeps stacked carefully in the mudroom at the entrance to his barn.

← ≪

Trey displays many objects from his family as well. He has his grandmother's baby shoe and his father's bronzed one; a gold piece that his grandfather gave his father "so he'd never be considered a vagrant"; and his grandfather's razor and knife from World War I.

≫ →

The wax wig form that sits near Trey's kitchen has glass eyes and real eyelashes. Trey found her at the Armory Show in New York and likes to put her in different hats for holidays.

DAVID EPSTEIN

Dogs—living and decorative—play a big role in David and Wade's life together as well as in the decor of both their Sag Harbor weekend house they bought and renovated in 2005 (pictured here) and in their West Village apartment.

Two cast-iron bulldogs from a local antiques shop guard the fireplace in their Sag Harbor house. Ten years ago, it was possible to score deals in Hamptons vintage shops, but according to David, that ship has sailed.

At age six, David Blair Epstein came home from the pool one day, still dripping, and made himself comfy on his mom's carved wooden Chinese dragon chair. "You can still see the little tush mark from my wet bathing suit," he said. "I don't know if it's an antique or if it's even old, but everyone in the family knew it was where David got in trouble when he was six."

But now the chair—tush mark and all—is out of that suburban Kansas City attic where it had been relegated after the incident and sits in the entry of the large one-bedroom apartment David shares with his partner, Wade Tajerian, in Manhattan's West Village.

David, who got into Internet advertising and marketing in 1995, proudly decorates his homes with several chairs that once caused pain. The couple's Sag Harbor house that they renovated in 2005 sits on a cove and holds much of the Dunbar furniture that David's mother and grandmother amassed throughout the 1970s and '80s—including two precarious upholstered armchairs. "When you leaned even slightly forward, you'd fall right out," he recalled. "Grandma despised those chairs from the first time she fell, so she gave them to my mother. My mom fell, too, and handed them down to me." David took them to a local Kansas City upholstery shop, whose customers had been tumbling from these chairs for ages. The staff knew a trick: add a brick to the back before applying the fabric to balance out the weight. Now those chairs flank the French doors that lead to the patio, each covered in baby-blue upholstery, sporting a well-placed brick. No one's fallen out since.

Both the Sag Harbor house and their apartment in the city are arranged with a keen decorator's eye, a mix of classic, linear, upholstered pieces and mid-century furniture—all of it simple, clean, comfortable (now that the chairs are fixed).

Twentieth-century art and photography fill the walls of both their weekday and weekend homes. David snapped up Steve Schapiro's large-scale black-and-white photo of a woman at the beach reading the paper with a headline screaming out THE WORST IS YET TO COME because that "is always my natural instinct and thinking." It hangs in the living room of their apartment, directly above his uncle's black leather Eames chair and ottoman that he'd begged for since boyhood and below a Rodney Smith photo of a man in a trench coat peeking over an ivy-covered wall.

"I bought that one because it completely reminded me of the Hamptons," he said of Smith's 1994 photo. "Maybe because I'm a Midwesterner and not really from New York, I never really felt that I needed to be a part of the whole 'keeping up with the Joneses' and 'the grass is always greener on the other side' thing that happens out in the Hamptons. But I certainly saw it when I moved out there, and I loved that this photograph caught the sentiment perfectly."

For the walls of the Sag Harbor house, he and Wade chose modernist, abstract paintings that David's grandparents had brought back from a trip to Havana in the 1950s. "I think they just bought them from artists who'd set up little stalls along the beach," David said. "My mom couldn't stand them, but I loved how they came from the pre-Castro days when Cuba was more of a wild place. I found them and had them framed—and they're framed in my brain as special moments with my family."

While many people inherit and treasure their relatives' beloved possessions, David has gone out of his way to fill his two homes with the pieces his family loathed—and he loves every piece of it.

»—↑

The Sag Harbor house
holds much of the Dunbar
furniture that David's
mother and grandmother
amassed throughout the
1970s and '80s—including
two precarious upholstered
armchairs that much of
his family despised.

Abstract paintings that
David's grandparents
brought back from Havana
in the 1950s fill many of
the walls at the couple's
weekend home.

←⫷

The entry to the couple's West Village apartment is filled out with a Korean War army desk, stripped and polished to a high shine, on which sits an old airplane propeller and a loosely modeled Italian bust lamp draped with colorful medals.

⫸→

Whether in the city apartment or the weekend house on the cove, David and Wade maintain a clean, calming, and very comfortable aesthetic. This barley-twist armchair sits under the stairs of the Sag Harbor house, just off the expansive, white, marble-laden kitchen.

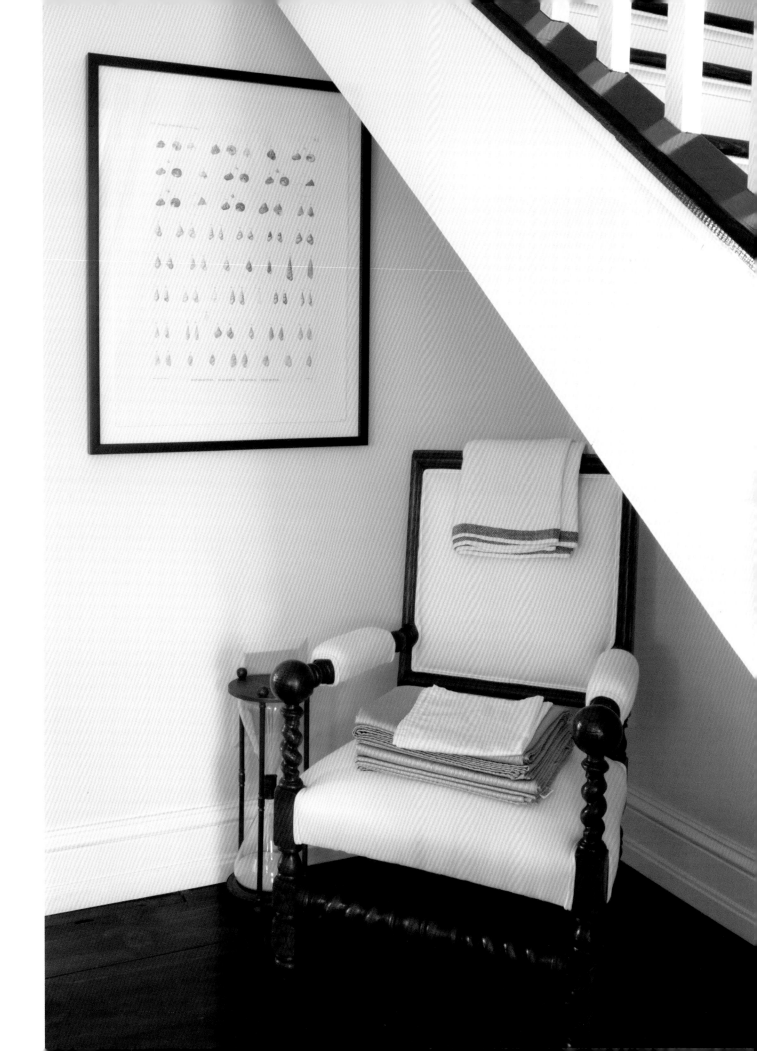

>>→

In the living room of the couple's Greenwich Village apartment, Gus, their Maltese-Yorkie mix, sits nestled on a black leather Eames chair that belonged to David's uncle. David snapped up Steve Schapiro's large-scale black-and-white photo of a woman at the beach reading the paper with a headline screaming out THE WORST IS YET TO COME because that "is always my natural instinct and thinking."

>>→

The small cast-iron Jack Russell comes from Wade's family; they have always owned living, breathing, barking versions of those wiry little terriers.

← ⫷

At age six, David came home
from the pool and made
himself comfy on his mom's
carved wooden Chinese
dragon chair—and ruined
the seat with a little tush
mark. The family relegated it
to the attic, but he rescued
it and placed it in the entry
of his New York apartment.

⫸ →

Wade started running
marathons at age forty as
a way to ignore his doctors
and self-heal a bad back. His
back is now fine, and evidence of his races is draped
around the neck of their
Italian lamp in the entry.

David and Wade like to invest in art by local artists and friends. The abstract purple-and-white painting that hangs in their living room is by New York painter Bo Joseph.

The 1950s Cuban abstract paintings from David's grandparents crop up all over the Sag Harbor house.

NAIDA MCSHERRY

Naida McSherry, a queen of Brooklyn real estate, has always found beauty in the ratty, well used, and worn out. She built a career around bringing new life to old houses by connecting them to worthy, caring owners. And she's built a life giving well-loved and very well-used objects a new context inside her own home, a two-story converted carriage house in the heart of Clinton Hill, the Brooklyn neighborhood she's adored for almost three decades.

Naida's home houses her countless collections: relics from old science labs, scores of trophies, paraphernalia from old political campaigns, and mementoes from her epic travels. This carriage house of curiosities tells a story of her life and taste for the old and discarded that she's had since she was a young girl growing up outside Chicago.

During college, Naida toyed with the concept of running for office but chose instead to pursue her artistic side, landing a job designing high-end fabrics in New York. She settled in Greenwich Village in the late 1960s, when the area was ripe with protests and Bob Dylan and the Beats. "At the time, you didn't move to New York to move to Brooklyn," she said. But even then, in the midst of all the bohemian rhapsody and relative roughness of the area compared to what the Village is today, Naida felt priced out of her own neighborhood within a few years. So always up for an adventure, she headed five miles east, and discovered block after tree-lined block of old, slightly decayed mansions and brownstones that nineteenth-century tycoons had built for their families. She'd arrived in Clinton Hill and there was no going back.

She found a house and fell in love with the process of the property search, especially when the residences were filled with light and space and crown moldings and marble fireplaces and layer upon layer of history. Infected with the real estate bug and the thrill of matching other pioneering people to these neglected architectural beauties, she gave up her design work and became a broker. By the end of her twenty-two-year career in real estate, she estimates that she'd matched families with over four hundred homes in Clinton Hill and the adjoining neighborhood, Fort Greene. She only took on clients who impressed her with their respect for the homes and an eagerness to create a community in these neighborhoods over the long term. "The big brokers who are here now wouldn't even touch these neighborhoods," she said. "I had a tremendous impact on this neighborhood. This was my neighborhood. I wanted to fit the houses with the people. I wanted them to appreciate the houses."

Inside her two-story carriage house on a quiet, tree-lined street, she juxtaposes the objects in her own beloved collections that come together to evoke her fiercely independent spirit, love of community, and political pride.

Miniature replicas of real houses—an homage to her love of real estate—sit on tables and hang from the walls like floating sculptures. Two large taxidermied pelicans—decommissioned from the Brooklyn Museum's collection—stand proudly on the edge of the living room and "Ngandi," a warthog mount she found in an antiques shop in Cape Town watches out from across the room. Rescued lockers and bookcases from the tragically demolished labs and classrooms at a small college in the neighborhood hold yarns and rusted oilcans. "I don't care about anything being valuable," she said. "I buy things because I think they're interesting."

There's also her wonderful photography, which captures her worldly adventures in China, Egypt, Antarctica—and Iowa. Always political, she and a group headed to Des Moines in 1960 to follow the Kennedy campaign in Iowa. "We were sitting at the table next to John F. Kennedy. I sat right by Lyndon Johnson and rode an elevator with [the economist and Kennedy advisor] John Galbraith. It was a great time." Her remarkable, close-up, black-and-white photos of these Democratic titans from that pivotal weekend cover the walls of her stairway, placed beneath an old beaded African elephant head—providing a cheeky sense of political balance.

Her coffee table serves as a display case for hundreds of mementoes from political races past and tiny celluloid trinkets from advertising campaigns of decades past, not far from her expansive collection of vintage trophies that she found at an auction, including one that a couple scored for dancing the best jitterbug in the Far Rockaways during World War II.

While most of her prized possessions hang and sit casually out in the open, she has taken care to protect many of her pieces inside glass cabinets, including the Civil War medical equipment from the Brattleboro Retreat mental hospital, founded in 1834 as the Vermont Asylum for the Insane. In need of funding a few years back, the current administration auctioned off the contents of its attic and Naida bought a carload of Gladstone bags, splints, anatomy charts, and a wicker coffin.

Of all the things she's found over the years, it may be that coffin that stays with her the longest. Naida has already staked out her eternal piece of real estate and has ensured that her surroundings look just as she planned. She will be buried in that coffin, she says. In Brooklyn.

← ⋘ ← ⋘

Inside her two-story carriage house on a quiet, treelined street in Clinton Hill, Brooklyn, Naida juxtaposes objects in her own beloved collections that come together to evoke her fiercely independent spirit, love of community, and political activism. Of all the things she's found over the years, it may be the wicker coffin on top of the illuminated shelves that stays with her longest. She will be buried in that coffin, she says. In Brooklyn.

← ⋘

Naida has been traveling to Vermont with friends for years, and now owns a second home there, in Putney. The local vintage shops and auctions have supplied her with much of her collection, including the signs from an old Vermont vacation retreat that hang over her bed.

←«←«

Most of Naida's expansive vintage trophy collection came from a single auction in Vermont. Her favorite is a prize for a couple who danced the best jitterbug in the Far Rockaways during World War II.

»→

Naida has collected canes from all over, but her favorites are the carnival canes with the little dog heads. Others are "just canes," she says. The painting is by Canadian artist Gathie Falk.

»→

At flea markets in Brooklyn, Vermont, and along her other travels, Naida scoops up old frames and black-and-white photos and then pairs them up.

←‹‹‹

Naida began to amass
her doll collection as an
adult, appreciating them
as objects that have been
worn, tattered, and loved
during their existence. Her
collection dates back more
than a century and ranges
from handmade folk rag
dolls to celluloid versions
from the 1920s and 1930s.

›››→

"Ngandi," a warthog mount
she found in an antiques
shop in Cape Town, was held
prisoner by the Department
of Agriculture upon arriving
at New York's JFK Airport
in a crate with all her
other finds from the trip.
Eventually he made it to his
new home on Naida's living
room wall in Clinton Hill.

›››→

Lockers rescued from the
demolished labs and classrooms of a small college in
the neighborhood hold her
collection of rusted oilcans,
most of which she picked up
in Vermont over the years.
"I don't care about anything
being valuable," she said.
"I buy things because I
think they're interesting."

←«
Two large taxidermied pelicans—decommissioned from the Brooklyn Museum's collection—stand proudly on the edge of the living room.

←«
Miniature replicas of real houses—an homage to her love of real estate—sit on tables and hang from the walls like floating sculptures throughout the carriage house.

← ≪

Like the lockers, Naida rescued these cubby shelves from a demolished college in her neighborhood. An old Helene Curtis apparatus that used to give women permanents stands next to it, along with a framed cover of LOOK magazine depicting a woman with the contraption affixed to her hair. The headline cries out, TORTURES WOMEN ENDURE TO BE BEAUTIFUL.

≫ →

Naida assumes that this eight-foot-tall panel came from a VFW hall. It lists the names of American soldiers who died in World War II.

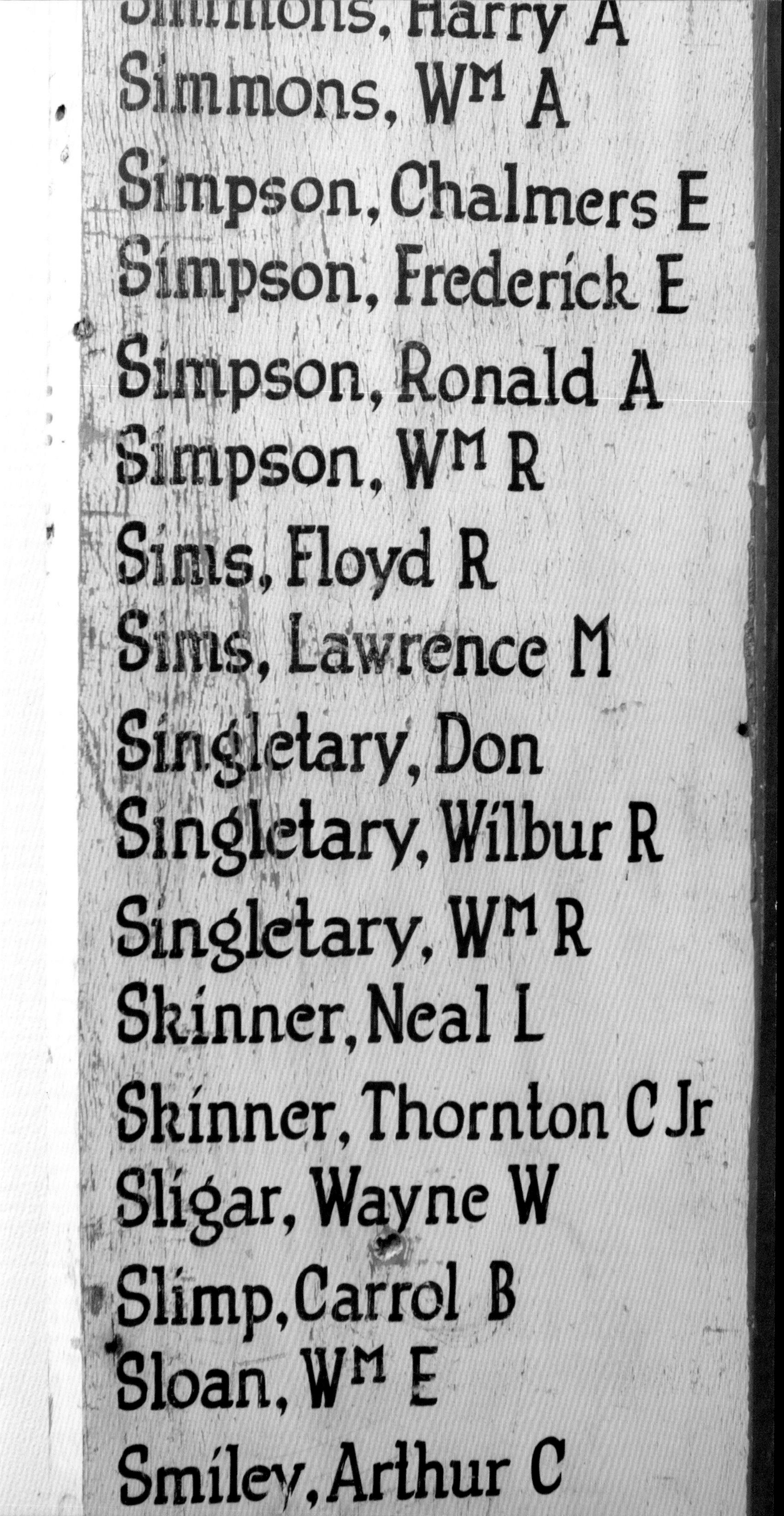

Simmons, Harry A
Simmons, Wm A
Simpson, Chalmers E
Simpson, Frederick E
Simpson, Ronald A
Simpson, Wm R
Sims, Floyd R
Sims, Lawrence M
Singletary, Don
Singletary, Wilbur R
Singletary, Wm R
Skinner, Neal L
Skinner, Thornton C Jr
Sligar, Wayne W
Slimp, Carrol B
Sloan, Wm E
Smiley, Arthur C

←—◄◄

In need of funding a few
years back, the Brattleboro
Retreat mental hospital
(founded in 1834 as the
Vermont Asylum for the
Insane), auctioned off
the contents of its attic
and Naida bought a carload
of Gladstone bags, splints,
anatomy charts, and the
wicker coffin that sits on
top of these shelves.

►►—↑

Naida has been politically
minded her whole life and
even ran for public office
when she was in college.
Her remarkable black-and-
white photos of Democratic
leaders during the 1960
Kennedy campaign cover
the walls of her stairway.

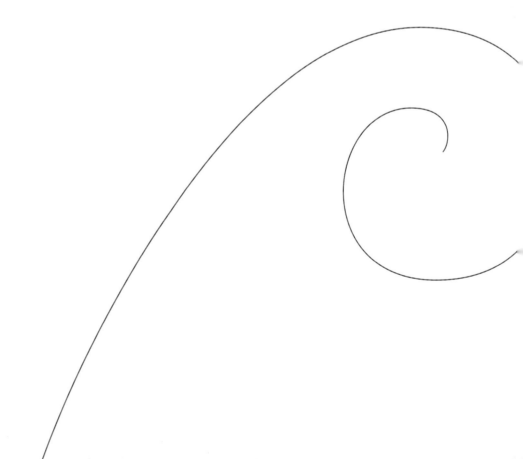

JESSICA WARREN

Just close your eyes and run your hand across the rack until you hit good fabric. That's how Jessica Warren can shop thrift stores. Blind.

She learned this skill from her grandfather. He was a leader of the Saint Vincent de Paul Society in suburban Detroit. Part of his duties included emptying out the drop boxes of clothing donated for the charity's secondhand shops. "Looking back on it now, this probably violated a bunch of rules, but my grandfather used to open the door to the drop boxes and let us go into them to sift through all the stuff," she said. "We would be sitting on mounds of bags, taking what we wanted. My sister took all things lacy, while I'd be exclaiming, 'Ohhh! Cashmere!' We always went for the great materials."

Jessica and her sister Rachel became the "ultimate thrifting team," she said. "We comb over a store in a way that alarms other shoppers." This resourcefulness, patience, and taste for quality textiles, combined with a childhood full of lessons from her mother and grandmother in ironing, crocheting, embroidery, macramé, cooking, baking, and even cutting hair, set her apart and played a huge role in the woman—and professional interior decorator—she would become.

"I feel like I'm part of the last generation of women who were raised to be housewives with domestic skills that have long since gone out of favor," Jessica said. "Living in New York, I don't know a lot of women who were taught those kinds of skills. So many women I know can't cook or do these practical things any longer. I was raised in a self-sufficient kind of world. Of course you use toothpaste to get a ring out of a table."

To say she's a modern-day June Cleaver, though, is like referring to Hillary Clinton simply as a First Lady. And her home is about as far from 1950s suburbia as Versailles.

In 2007, she and her husband, Doug, bought a run-down 25-foot-wide, 10,000-square-foot Queen Anne mansion in Clinton Hill, Brooklyn, for their family, including their daughter, Sophia, and son, Will. Built in 1887 as a private residence by Charles Erhart, co-founder of the pharmaceutical giant Pfizer, it was later used by the Brooklyn Public Library and a Catholic girls' school, and eventually even housed a punk-rock nightclub in the basement.

The couple enlisted Neuhaus Design Architecture to painstakingly bring this mansion back to her former glory in a way never envisioned by the architects who designed it in the late nineteenth century. The elaborate parquet and inlaid wood floors were repaired and custom-stained, as were the plaster moldings in most of the rooms. The front parlor and the master bedroom directly above gleam with light and an airiness that would never have seemed possible with all the heavy wood and dim lighting associated with architecture at the turn of the last century.

Jessica felt strongly that the integrity and legacy of this beautiful structure should remain intact, yet she wanted it to be a family home—and for the entire house to tell a story. She has approached the furnishings in the same way. The furniture throughout comes mostly from Jessica's decades of thrifting, much of it restored or enhanced with beautiful new upholstery or finishes. The colors used through the house create wildly different moods from room to room. Move back from the bright white front parlor toward the living room area, and the atmosphere darkens cozily with elaborate mahogany moldings and muted gray walls, a perfect foil to the refined, late mid-century furniture that fills the room.

There are three-legged chairs that support the sitter's back with a simple, elegant piece of bent wood that she bought online from a small antiques dealer. In lieu of a coffee table, she chose textured yet polished petrified-wood stumps, each weighing more than a small child. She found those at the discount megastore, HomeGoods, for one hundred dollars a pop. She knew what they normally go for so she stocked up in a spree. "I love a little nature in a room. I think I bought about seven that day. My husband, Doug, joked that the wheels were going to bend right off the shopping cart." The whole house is a study in contrasts: ornate meets deceptively simple; old meets new; rough meets smooth. "As a rule, I cannot see a curve without a straight line and I cannot see black without white," she said.

This juxtaposition is particularly evident in Jessica's favorite room of refuge: the master bath. Larger than the first studios of many twenty-something New Yorkers, the room boasts soaring ceilings, a working fireplace, and solid wood moldings. Smack in the middle of the room sits a gigantic, modern, oval tub from Ovo. "The edges of the tub are so fine, it feels like I'm bathing in a gigantic tea cup," she said. During her daily soaks, she looks out at the hand-painted de Gournay Chinoiserie bird-and-tree-print wallpaper that she'd dreamed of having her whole life and up at the prized nickel half-sphere and crystal Baccarat chandelier, which she found years ago at a kitschy potpourri-and-fairy-costume shop in Michigan.

She hopes that Sophia, Will, and the kids they might have someday will want these treasures (and the stories that go along with them). But she's filled the years leading up to the time when she will hand down her prized possessions by passing on her love and talent for the hunt. "I don't know that my kids would describe their early days in thrift stores as learning experiences—probably more like torture! But they did learn, and now they both are excellent treasure hunters. Sophia wears vintage clothes and already decorates in a 'collected' way. Will has a very discerning eye. He can spot quality a mile away!"

←—⫷←—⫷

In 2007, Jessica and Doug Warren bought a run-down 25-foot-wide, 10,000-square-foot Queen Anne mansion in Clinton Hill, Brooklyn, and embarked on a painstaking restoration. While the architecture is grand by normal standards, the Warrens are exceedingly laid-back; they allow scores of guests and their dogs—Muggle (seen here) and Klaus—to roam freely.

←—⫷

Jessica and Doug's son, Will, is a fan of artist Kehinde Wiley, whom he met in 2007. In the years since, the Warrens acquired Wiley's busts, *Louis XVI, The Sun King* (left) and *St. Francis of Adelaide* (right).

»→

The master bedroom boasts
a balcony and a working
fireplace. What was once
a dark, somber room has
been lightened up with
blond bleached moldings
and a soft palette of
pinks, grays, and beige.
The sofa is one piece of
a large pink Sally Sirkin
Lewis sectional that Jessica
found at a thrift shop in
Brooklyn. She reuphol-
stered it in beige suede.

»→

While checking out at a thrift
store in Florida, Jessica
saw this abstract sculpture
displayed behind the counter
and snapped it up. After
investigating, she discovered it was by Curtis Jeré,
a well-known collaboration
between modernist sculptors
Jerry Fels and Curtis Freiler.

←◀◀

Jessica bought this pair of three-legged chairs, which support the sitter's back with a simple, elegant piece of bent wood, online from a small antiques dealer. In lieu of a coffee table, she chose two textured yet polished petrified-wood stumps, each weighing more than a small child, for the living room area. She found the stumps at HomeGoods and stocked up, buying more than a half dozen.

▶▶▶→

Jessica and Doug took Will to a party in Kehinde Wiley's studio in 2007 where Will was moved by Wiley's painting *Encourage Good Manners and Politeness; Bright Up Your Surroundings with Plants*—which now hangs in the dining room. The Garland chandelier by Studiolo was one of Jessica's big splurges and helps to balance the unusually long parlor floor.

←—⫷

Jessica salvaged and pre-
served many of the house's
light fixtures that now hang
in a cluster in the family's
sprawling basement. Prior to
the start of the renovation,
her teenage daughter (with
the help of her brother) organized all-ages punk shows
in that space. The basement
also includes a wine cellar, a
guest bath, and a TV room
with glazed brick walls that
are original to the house.

Jessica nabbed a set of silver-colored carved doors that resemble the work of 1970s furniture designer Paul Evans. She hired a woodworker to convert them into a credenza and when he started to clean the panels, the color changed dramatically; he soon realized that he was washing away years of nicotine. They decided to stop all of the cleaning and match the rest of the wood to the panels instead.

In a last-minute attempt to furnish the library before the arrival of visiting relatives, Jessica hit her favorite Brooklyn thrift shops in Bed-Stuy and Park Slope, where she picked up velvet chairs, a vintage Sergio Asti floor lamp, and this onyx coffee table.

»⌐

Larger than the first studio
apartments of many twenty-
something New Yorkers,
the master bath—Jessica's
favorite room of refuge—
boasts soaring ceilings, a
working fireplace, and solid
wood moldings. Smack in
the middle of the room sits
a gigantic, modern, oval tub
from Ovo. "The edges of
the tub are so fine, it feels
as though I'm bathing in a
gigantic tea cup," she said.

←«

During her daily soaks,
Jessica looks out at
the hand-painted de
Gournay Chinoiserie
bird-and-tree-print wall-
paper that she dreamed
of having her entire life.

SEAN MACPHERSON

The Navajo intentionally weave a mistake into every one of their blankets, eliminating an expectation for perfection in the end. That philosophy could also be used to describe how Sean MacPherson has designed all his restaurants and hotels, as well as the fire-damaged, nineteenth-century West Village butcher shop that he gutted and renovated with salvaged wood and fixtures to make into his three-story family home.

Over the last two decades, Sean has brought that vision to a series of hotels and restaurants like the Jane, the Bowery, the Maritime, and the Waverly Inn in New York, the Crow's Nest in Montauk, and some of Los Angeles's hippest eateries. Each project manages to usher in an entirely new kind of meaning of hospitality and comfort away from home. The lobbies invite lounging with a book, an issue of *The New Yorker*, or an artisanal cocktail.

"Most of my colleagues tend to hire design firms," Sean said. "I design and build all of my own places. I always love places that feel personal, like the owner made them. I love that there's the humanity of an individual making it and having the vision, not an outside professional team."

Even though many of his existing projects are in New York, Sean approaches everything with a West Coast sensibility instilled in him throughout his childhood in Malibu, Mexico, and Sun Valley, Idaho. In the Jane, an old hotel for sailors and at one time a temporary home to Titanic survivors, Sean merged 1930s references with the famed L.A. hotel the Chateau Marmot and Hearst Castle, while the Maritime is pure mid-century nautical, referencing beach clubs, steamship travel, and the reading rooms of old seafarers. His nautically themed Crow's Nest Inn and Restaurant in Montauk offers weekenders and surfers a casual, unfussy retreat.

"I feel very much from the West," he said. "The young years leave their fingerprints on you, and for me, it's all California and the West. I'm not overly nostalgic, but you inevitably bring your past with you."

Sean was born in New Zealand, the child of two champion surfers. His father, a native New Zealander, was in the classic surf film *The Endless Summer* and met his mother while touring to promote the movie. His mom, now in her mid-seventies, still surfs every day. She grew up in San Francisco, the daughter of a Scottish businessman—who, along with his brothers, owned one of the largest leather distributors and saddleries on the West Coast.

Sean's parents split when he was a young boy, and his mother took him to America. Within a few years, she met and fell in love with Earl Thornburg, a rugged man from a ranching family, whose cowboy brother became one of the Marlboro men who appeared in ads for the cigarette brand. They never married, but Thornburg became a father figure to Sean and helped ingrain in him a deep appreciation for life in the West.

Sean spent his early twenties in Los Angeles, surfing and developing and designing restaurants. He came east over a decade ago and found his current home in 2008. "It might have been the last great opportunity in the West Village, but it wasn't some secret deal," he said. A fire had torn through the butcher shop, leaving just half the roof. Only a couple of the original mid-nineteenth-century chimneys could be salvaged. "The building sat here for sale for two to three years. I think people were just afraid of it."

He wanted to keep it as a ruin, like Miss Havisham's place in *Great Expectations*, but the building department wouldn't allow it. "I at least wanted to restore it to something original," he said. "I love all the organic elbowroom of the West, but love the history of the East Coast. I wanted to live in something that felt like New York City. I think it's important wherever you live for the environment to feel like you're in that place, even if there are references elsewhere."

Sean added salvaged wide plank wood to the floors, vintage brass fixtures and slabs of white marble to the bathrooms, and marble mantels to the three fireplaces. A huge nineteenth-century bookcase with doors covers an entire wall of the living room, filled with hundreds of coffee-table books arranged akimbo, perfectly imperfect. A huge rough wood table holds the dinners that he and his wife, Rachelle Hruska, prepare in their kitchen, which has Spanish tiled walls and vintage seafoam-green appliances. They often grill outside on the large patio with more Spanish tile, a table that seats ten, and walls overflowing with herbs, flowers, and wildly growing plants. Photos of his mom surfing reside on the mantel. A MacPherson western saddle—from his grandfather's leather goods company—rides the mahogany banister, across from a series of matching watercolor portraits of world leaders like Winston Churchill and Mohandas Gandhi and notable faces, like California senator Alan Cranston, that hang salon style up all three floors of the stairway. "I found those in 1989 when I was opening my first restaurant, Olive," he said. "I was twenty-five years old. I had no time and no money. But I had this enormous wall to fill. So I went to the Long Beach flea market and saw some frames sticking out from under this big box. I lifted it up and found this pile of paintings. They were strangely perfect." Sean asked the price. "Twenty-five," he was told.

"You never know what that means at a flea market. Were they $25 each or $2,500?" They were $25—for the whole lot. And they became the centerpiece of the restaurant. Sean closed Olive years ago after a battle with the landlord, but these paintings, which have been his for nearly a quarter century, are now what greets visitors and friends to his West Village house.

Sean didn't tackle his home as a historical renovation, but rather as an effort to embody a feeling that he associated with old New York, a tough town that's always achieved greatness despite—or because of—its grime and grit and grunge and countless imperfections.

"We all love our friends and accept their flaws because they're what make them special and human," he said. "I want all my projects to be as human and personal as possible. Hopefully you can feel some sort of humanity behind the mistakes."

←‹‹←‹‹

A huge nineteenth-century bookcase covers an entire wall of Sean's living room, filled with hundreds of coffee-table books arranged akimbo, perfectly imperfect.

←—⫷←—⫷

The stairway is lined with
a series of watercolor
portraits of world leaders
like Winston Churchill and
Mohandas Gandhi. These
used to cover an entire wall
of Olive, Sean's first restaurant, which he opened in L.A.
in 1989. He bought the whole
set at a Long Beach flea market for twenty-five dollars.

⫸—→

Sean installed this swing
in his living room as a nod
to the great New York
architect Stanford White,
who had a swing in his
24th Street apartment.

←—«

Sean was born in New Zealand, the child of two champion surfers. His mom (in the photo on the left), now in her mid-seventies, still surfs every day.

←—«

Sean's mother grew up in San Francisco, the daughter of a Scottish businessman who, along with his brothers, owned one of the largest leather distributors and saddleries on the West Coast. This hand-tooled Western saddle from his family's company hangs over the banister.

202

»⟶
A detail of the MacPherson saddle. Sean's maternal grandfather, Kenneth, from whom he got his middle name, headed the MacPherson leather distribution operations in San Francisco, while each of the other brothers ran the Seattle, Portland, Los Angeles, and San Diego outposts.

←—◀◀
Sean found the "Mean
Motherfuckers" motorcycle
belt at a flea market and
has made it an heirloom-in-
waiting for his son, Maxwell.

←—◀◀
The "heirloom-in-waiting"
sits in front of a vintage
leather hippo. Sean has a
much larger hippo standing
behind the sofa and has
used them in his hotel decor.

ACKNOWLEDGMENTS

We made this book for our sweet, wonderful mom who taught us how important it is to think with a strong, enduring, and independent vision when shopping, and that every investment (small and large) should be worth saving and using for the rest of our lives—and worthy of passing on.

We owe so much to all of the wonderful individuals, couples, and families featured in this book, who opened their beautiful homes and rich histories to us. Craftsmanship, materials, and artistry may make objects valuable; it's the human touch, the stories, and the provenance that make them priceless. They helped show this.

We'd also like to thank our dad for all the years he spent reading us stories of monkeys and elephants before bed every night, and telling his own tales of adventure that have inspired so much of our taste and passions; Auntie Rae for carrying on our mom's legacy and supporting us at every step; Alida Morgan for her honesty, humor, and incredible circle of friends; Aunt Carey for being a catalyst and proud preservationist of her family's past; Patricia Shackelford for the spark that set this project off; Jean Sagendorph Pocker for her strategic matchmaking and brilliant negotiations; Alicia Cheng and Tom Wilder of MGMT. design for their aesthetic vision; Bradford Robotham for his perfectionism and enhancements; Elizabeth Smith for her flawless attention to detail; and especially Caitlin Leffel, for her illuminating edits, diplomacy, and unwavering patience and calm.

GLADE TAXI CORP

»→⌐

Our mom and dad
saying goodbye to
their guests after their
wedding reception
in 1975.

First published in the United States in 2013
by Rizzoli International Publications, Inc.
300 Park Avenue South
New York, NY 10010
www.rizzoliusa.com

Designed by MGMT. design

Rizzoli Editor: Caitlin Leffel

ISBN: 978-0-8478-3959-9
Library of Congress Number: 2012948953

2013 2014 2015 2016
10 9 8 7 6 5 4 3 2 1

Printed in China